PONY

In the same series

PONY WATCH
Elinore Havers

A PONY TO CATCH
Elinore Havers

PONY PAGEANT
Sylvia Scott White

By the same author
in the Crown Pony hardbacks series

PONIES ACROSS THE RIVER

THE MERRY-MARCH PONIES

PONY SLEUTHS

by

ELINORE HAVERS

LUTTERWORTH PRESS
GUILDFORD AND LONDON

First published in the Crown Pony hardback series 1966

This paperback edition first published 1975

ISBN 0 7188 2190 4

The Publishers are grateful to Miss J. Kemp of Mounters Farm, Chawton, Hampshire, for permission to take the cover photograph at her riding stable

PRINTED OFFSET LITHO AND BOUND IN GREAT BRITAIN
BY COX & WYMAN LTD
LONDON, FAKENHAM AND READING

CONTENTS

CHAPTER ONE

A PONY TO LOOK AFTER

THE first thing to do to start any holidays properly is to change into old clothes, so Janet Craig dropped her school hat, with its green and white band, on her bed and began to undo her green and white striped tie. Once she was in jeans and an old jersey she'd feel school was over for a bit—not that boarding school wasn't fun, but it was heavenly to be home. She opened her suitcase to fish out her sandals and then she ran downstairs, leaving the suitcase on the floor with various garments spilling out from it.

At tea, a particularly good one with her favourite chocolate cake, Janet told her mother about the end of term festivities. She changed the subject when asked about her report and said, "A girl at school, Susan Fenton, has come to live near here. She's in my House and my form. Can we go and see the Fentons tomorrow?"

"We might ask Susan to tea," Mrs. Craig suggested. "Has she any brothers or sisters?"

"Two brothers, the lucky thing!"

"Where have they come to live?"

"The other side of Trewsbury. Quite near us."

"Oh splendid!" Mrs. Craig said. "It will be nice for you to have someone to do things with, as there's nobody just your age near here."

"When can we go?" Janet asked. "They've got ponies and I'm longing to see them."

"I'll write to Mrs. Fenton and ask them to tea. What's the name of their house?" But Janet could not remember. Only that it was near Trewsbury and had a paddock.

"They won't be in the telephone book yet, if they've only just come, but we could ask at the post office next time we go to Trewsbury," Mrs. Craig said. She was stacking tea things on the trolley. Janet pushed it to the kitchen where she found Goloshes asleep on the chair which was called Goloshes' chair. He had his tail wrapped round to cover his front paws.

"Beautiful boy!" Janet picked him up and cuddled him. As soon as he was awake he sprang down, stretched in the way that Janet called "like a croquet hoop" and rubbed against her legs purring loudly. "He's marvellously clean. His shirt front and his stockings absolutely snow-white and his coat and feet so shiny black, just like goloshes," Janet said admiringly. "Lovely to see him again. Only I wish he was a pony! Mummy, I think I'll get my bike out and go and see Mr. Timms and Laddie."

"Oh dear," Mrs. Craig said, "Mr. Timms is ill. He was taken to hospital yesterday. Quite suddenly. I heard about it this morning from the grocer's man."

"Oh, poor Mr. Timms!" Janet said. "What's the matter with him? Is he very ill?"

"I didn't hear any details," replied her mother. "But he may not be very bad. He'd have to go into hospital if he was ill, to be looked after, as he lives alone. I don't think he has any relatives."

"Who'll look after Laddie?" Janet asked. "Mummy, could we go and see him and find out about Laddie? And how Mr. Timms is," she added.

"Yes. We could visit him tomorrow afternoon," Mrs. Craig said. "And we could make inquiries about where the Fentons live when we go through Trewsbury. Poor Mr. Timms! Such a nice, obliging little man."

Mr. Timms lived in a tiny cottage, all by himself, quite near the Craigs. His pony Laddie pulled a little cart and Mr. Timms went round selling vegetables and fruit. Mrs. Craig always bought from him and he was a great friend of Janet's. He had worked with horses all his life and had done a lot of interesting things which Janet liked hearing about. He'd been a jockey when he was young but he'd got too heavy and had taken a job as groom to a gentleman who drove a coach with four horses. He'd been in the cavalry and he'd broken in young horses and schooled show jumpers. He had lots of stories about horses and he often gave Janet useful tips which helped her to improve her riding. She was very disappointed at not seeing him. But she could go and see Laddie.

She took three lumps of sugar and put them in her pocket. Mr. Timms didn't really approve of a lot of titbits for a pony but Janet thought he wouldn't mind this once; it was the first day of the holidays and besides, Laddie might be missing Mr. Timms so sugar would cheer him up.

She got her bicycle out of the garage which adjoined the house. It was a new one which she had bought with her savings last holidays. It was a very nice shade of blue, it had three speeds and a basket on the handlebars, besides a cyclometer which told you how far you had been. It was rather dusty so she wiped it all over with a hanky which had been in her jeans pocket since last holidays and was very grubby. She had to blow up both tyres a little, but with the big fat pump it did not take long. Then she wheeled it out of the gate on to the road.

The Craigs' house was a small, modern one called Deneway (nobody knew why) and it had a tiny garden in the front and a larger one at the back. It was in a road with a lot of other houses all like it but a tiny bit different. Janet thought Deneway was much the nicest.

It would be fun to have Sue Fenton living near, she thought as she bicycled down the road, as there was nobody who was any use for doing things with, either in their road or in Trewsbury. The children were either babies or toddlers or else were quite big and going to college. It would be exciting to see the Fentons' ponies. She wished she had one too so that she could ride with them. Marvellous to have a pony! Laddie worked in his cart every day and on Sundays he needed a rest, so he couldn't be ridden much. But Mr. Timms let her ride him bareback in the paddock for a short while sometimes.

Just as she was going to turn into the main road to go along to the lane leading to Mr. Timms' cottage Janet met her father coming home from Trewsbury where he worked. He stopped the car and she got off her bike and they said hello. Then, of course, Janet went home with him, biking her fastest to try to keep up. So she didn't see Laddie after all. But she ate the sugar so it shouldn't be wasted.

Her father said she'd grown. Then he asked how she'd done in the end of term exams and Janet said regretfully but truthfully, "Not very well. But I'm much better at tennis and I can swim a length in the pool."

"Jolly good," said her father, who quite saw that this was important news. "We'll go over to the sea for the day one week-end and do some swimming." The sea was not far off by car and a seaside picnic was one of Janet's favourite treats in summertime.

She told her father about the Fentons coming to live near Trewsbury and he said at once: "They bought a house called Fairfield. This side of Trewsbury. It's no distance from here." Mr. Craig worked at a house agent's and the house had been sold through them. He told Janet the telephone number and she rushed to ring up.

"Ask them to tea the day after tomorrow," said Mrs. Craig. "We'll be going out tomorrow if we're going to visit Mr. Timms in hospital."

It was funny hearing Susan Fenton's voice over the telephone when they had only parted that morning at school. She said their new house was super and the ponies were fine. She was longing to show them to Janet and Mrs. Fenton accepted the invitation for them all to come to tea. Something to look forward to, Janet thought, and we're going to see Mr. Timms tomorrow and that will be nice.

Next morning Janet picked a bunch of flowers to take him; she knew Mr. Timms liked flowers because he grew them in his garden. She made a big bunch of pink and white snapdragons, with several red roses which smelt lovely, and it looked very gay. Her mother suggested that he might like some eggs so Janet chose the brownest ones (everyone likes brown eggs best) from the ones in the larder which Mrs. Craig had bought from the milkman that morning. They also took some papers and magazines.

Mr. Timms was lying in bed looking very pale. He was very pleased to see them and delighted with the flowers and the eggs and the magazines. He said he liked a nice read when he'd plenty of time. He was very cheerful but Janet had a feeling that he was pretending to feel better than he really did. "I'll soon be back home," he said. "It's a wonder how they can put you right nowadays, no matter what's wrong. They'll soon have me as good as new!"

"If there's anything you want, or anything we can do, please let me know," said Mrs. Craig. She was very sorry for him, as he had no family or relatives.

"There is something," Mr. Timms said, and then he looked at Janet. "Could you keep an eye on Laddie? I been worrying about 'im though he's all right in the field as there's plenty o' keep and the pond never goes dry. But I don't like nobody seeing to 'im."

"Of course. I'd love to," Janet said eagerly. "I was wondering about him last night." Just in time she stopped saying that was why she wanted to come and see Mr. Timms! "As a matter of fact," she went on, "I was going to see him last night but I met Daddy coming home so I stopped."

"You were?" asked Mr. Timms, looking pleased. "That's real good of you. If you'd just keep an eye on him to see there's nothing wrong, that's all that's needed. And of course if you want to have a ride round the field you're welcome, he won't be getting worked for a bit." Mr. Timms sighed. "The rest'll do 'im good though."

"Thank you awfully. I won't ride him too much," Janet said, "and I'll look after him and see he's all right."

Mrs. Craig said she thought they ought to go soon after this so they said good-bye and left. "I am glad we came," Janet said as they went down the corridor which was very well polished and had a slight smell of disinfectant. "I can look after Laddie every day and ride him in the field. And Mr. Timms won't be worrying any more."

"Yes, it's a good thing we came. Poor little man, he hasn't anyone to turn to for help. And he looks ill. But I expect he'll soon pick up now he's being cared for."

"I'll go and see Laddie after tea," Janet said. She felt quite important at having charge of him. Really it would be almost as good as having a pony.

CHAPTER TWO

A MYSTERY ABOUT LADDIE

AFTER tea Janet got on her bicycle and set out for Mr. Timms' cottage. She went down the road past the other houses, and when she reached the road at the end, which went to Trewsbury, she rode along it a short way until she came to the lane leading to Mr. Timms' cottage. It was narrow and rather rough. The hedges were so high that she could not see into Laddie's field which was on one side of the lane. On the other side there was a small wood and there were no other houses. The lane petered out at the cottage but there was a path which went on and came out on a common. Janet had sometimes ridden Laddie as far as the common when Mr. Timms had let her have a longer ride than usual.

The gate into the field was opposite the cottage. Janet leaned her bicycle against the railings in front of the garden and went into the field. She called "Laddie, Lad, come on boy!" and she looked all round, but she couldn't see him.

It was a small field, but there was one place where the ground sloped downhill that you couldn't see from the gate. He must be there, sheltering from the flies by standing under the trees, and Janet walked across towards it. There was plenty of grass. He'd get fat without any work, so really it would be a good thing to ride him a little every day to keep him fit. She wanted Mr. Timms to think she had looked after him properly, it'd be something to be proud of if he said how well Laddie looked when he came home. And to have a pony to ride every day, even for a short time, would be marvellous. It was a pity there wasn't a saddle for him and only his driving bridle with string for reins. It hadn't blinkers, though, because Mr. Timms didn't hold with them, which was a good thing.

She'd have to look after his feet, she thought, as she went slowly across the field. Take him to a blacksmith perhaps, if Mr. Timms was away for long. Mr. Timms had said more than once how important it was not to neglect a horse's feet. Altogether there was a lot to be thought of when you were in charge of a pony.

She reached the end of the field, and to her surprise there was no pony standing under the trees or beside the pond. She looked all round and called again, imitating the way Mr. Timms called, "Laddie, c-o-o-p, c-o-o-p." He always came when he heard that. But he didn't come and he was nowhere to be seen. He wasn't in the field at all.

Janet felt a horrid sensation of heaviness in her tummy. She looked all round the field again to make sure. He had gone. He must be lost. But how?

She thought hard as she walked back to the gate, still looking about her in case she'd missed seeing him. Mr. Timms had been taken to hospital the day before Janet had come home from school. Three days ago. Laddie had been there then. Could someone have stolen him? Mr. Timms had put her in charge of him and he was gone.

She leaned on the gate, frowning as she thought about it. Laddie had gone. Got out of the field? He never had, she was sure of that, Mr. Timms kept the fence up pretty well. So he must have been stolen. What could she do? Ask Daddy, she decided, he'd know.

She felt almost like crying as she bicycled home. She'd been so looking forward to having Laddie to look after, almost as if he were her own, and now he was lost before she'd had time to look after him at all. Or have even one little ride on him. Not that that mattered in comparison with the awful fact that he was lost. It was lucky that Mr. Timms wasn't well enough to be coming home just yet so she'd have time to look for Laddie. It wasn't horrid to be glad he was still ill, or so she hoped, because she *must* get Laddie back before he came home.

She almost dropped her bike when she got home, just shoved it against the garage door without taking care not to scratch it although it was so new, and rushed indoors to find her father. It was the last straw when Mrs. Craig said he wasn't home yet. Mrs. Craig wasn't unduly alarmed when Janet told her Laddie was missing. She was not used to ponies and knew nothing about them. "I expect he's just strayed away," she said. "He'll probably be back in his field next time you go there."

"He's stolen, I'm sure."

"Oh, I don't think that's likely," Mrs. Craig replied cheerfully. "He's not a valuable pony, only just a little pony in a greengrocer's cart. Nobody would bother to steal him."

Janet agreed it was unlikely. It was show ponies, or very good show jumpers, or Arabs, that got stolen, she thought. But *where* was Laddie?

When her father came home, after what seemed ages and Janet was sure he was later than usual, she poured out the story almost before he had time to get indoors.

"If the pony's really missing," he said, "we had better tell the police. Are you sure he's gone? He's not lurking under some trees or in some bushes? We don't want to report his loss if he's somewhere near at hand all the time."

"He's not in the field. I looked everywhere," Janet said earnestly. "I made absolutely sure. I don't think he could have got out. The fence is very high. Prickly too."

"Someone's borrowed him?" suggested Mr. Craig.

"Mr. Timms would have told us if anyone was going to," Janet pointed out.

"M'm." Mr. Craig lit his pipe thoughtfully. "It does seem to be a bit of a mystery."

"Would you tell the police? *Please*, Daddy. It's so awful for him to be lost when Mr. Timms asked me to look after him."

"You can't help it, darling; he went away before you even saw him. It's not your fault," Mrs. Craig said in a comforting voice.

"It doesn't make it seem any better," Janet said. "He's lost. If only I'd gone to see him the night I got back from school, as I meant to, I'd know how long he'd been missing then."

"What's he like?" Mr. Craig asked, taking up the telephone book to look up the number of the Trewsbury police station.

"Chestnut. About twelve two. His mane and tail are rather light. Otherwise there's nothing special about him. But I'd know him anywhere," declared Janet.

Mr. Craig telephoned the Trewsbury police and Janet listened, only able to hear what her father said, which was annoying. "What did they say?" she asked when he put down the receiver.

"They'll let all the other police stations in this district know that a pony is missing," Mr. Craig answered. "If one's found they'll get in touch with us."

"Aren't they going to look for him?" Janet asked, disappointed, for she wanted something done to find Laddie, at once.

"There's no proof he was stolen," her father explained. "They said that ponies often stray. I expect they'll keep a look out for him."

"That's a fat lot of use," Janet fumed. "They ought to go and look for him. Find clues and track him down, otherwise we'll never get him back. Daddy, we *must* find him."

"I'm sure the police will find him in time," Mrs. Craig said soothingly.

"But they're not doing anything about it," Janet said furiously.

"You don't expect them to call in Scotland Yard, do you?" teased her father. "Give them a little time and they'll let us know when he turns up."

"I hate waiting for things," Janet said. "I do hope they ring up soon and say they've got him." Ponies loose on roads could get run down by lorries, she thought with anxiety.

But the police didn't ring up the next day, and by the afternoon Janet was fretting. "Surely they could have found him by now. They can't be looking for him. I'm going to look for him myself. I simply must find him."

"Really, Janet dear, you're being rather silly. He hasn't been missing for very long. The police could hardly have found him yet. Not if he'd strayed far." Mrs. Craig was rather vague about it but she imagined Laddie would be found in a field somewhere, or that he would return to his own field one day.

"But Mr. Timms may get better and come home before we've got Laddie," Janet said. "He simply loves Laddie, and it'd be dreadful if he was still lost. I *simply must* find him."

Then the Fentons arrived for tea and Janet rushed out to meet them.

CHAPTER THREE

"*SLEUTHS LTD!*"

JANET and Susan, after greeting each other with shrieks of joy, began to gabble about their school.

"Break it up, Sue, we don't want to have to listen to your school gossip," protested Colin. He was the eldest, tall, thin and dark. Paul was the youngest and was short and stocky, with a round face and wiry hair which stuck up in tufts.

"Okay, we won't talk shop now," said Susan. She was a little taller than Janet and had short hair which was brown and wavy. Her eyes were grey. Janet, whose hair was fair, had very blue eyes.

"I'm terrifically glad you've come to live near us," Janet said when the two mothers had gone indoors leaving the children in the garden. "Specially just now, because I want your help." She told them of Laddie's disappearance and how Mr. Timms was in hospital. "I simply must get Laddie back. As he asked me to look after him, it's too frightful for him to have got lost. And Mr. Timms is so fond of him that it'd be awful if he came home and found Laddie wasn't there. Besides, he couldn't earn his living without Laddie and the cart."

"Poor old man, it'd be rotten for him," Susan said sympathetically. "But Laddie might be anywhere. If he'd got out of his field one night and strayed, nobody would know where he came from."

"He might have gone for miles," Janet agreed, "as I don't know when he went, three days ago perhaps."

"The police?" asked Colin. Janet told them how her father had rung them up and what they had said. "They're not looking, just waiting for him to turn up. I'm going to start looking for him and I want you to help, please."

"We'll start a proper sleuth and work out what can have happened," Colin said enthusiastically.

"Sleuths Limited!" said Paul.

"Pony Sleuths," Susan exclaimed. "We specialize in pony crimes. Crimes done *to* ponies, I mean, not done *by* them."

"Let's have a look at the place he vanished from," Colin suggested. "And look for clues."

"Sleuthing. Good!" said Paul. But as they were about to start Mrs. Craig said it was tea time. Afterwards they walked to Mr. Timms' field.

"I wonder who saw Laddie in the field last?" Colin said thoughtfully. "Is there anyone who'd go past there regularly and notice if he wasn't there?"

Janet shook her head. Colin was going to be good at sleuthing, she thought. "The lane past his field goes to Mr. Timms' cottage. Nobody goes along it unless they're going to see him. I don't think he has many visitors as he's hardly got any friends. And no relations. I only got to know him through stopping to pat Laddie."

"Did shops deliver things for him?" Susan asked.

"I shouldn't think so. He went out in his cart every day so he bought what he wanted then," explained Janet.

"Postman?" suggested Colin.

'I shouldn't think he got many letters," Janet replied. "This is the lane," she said as they came to the turning.

Colin was looking at the ground. "I don't see any tyre marks and a horse-box, or lorry, would leave big ones."

"Honestly, it's not likely anybody came with a horse box to steal him," Janet said. "He's not a bit valuable."

"You've got to think of everything," Colin answered.

"Does Laddie ever get a stone in his hoof?" Paul asked, pulling a big knife out of his shorts pocket. "I had this for my birthday and it's got this thing for taking stones out of horses' hooves but none of our ponies ever gets one in."

"One of them's sure to pick up a stone one day," Susan said consolingly.

"I bet gypsies have got Laddie," said Paul.

"The first thing to do is to see if he could have got out," Colin announced. So they walked all round the field examining the fence. They found one weak spot where a determined pony might have pushed through into the lane but as the ground was hard there were no hoof marks to show if Laddie had gone that way.

They walked round the cottage, admiring Mr. Timms' flowers. Then they went round to the back and saw Laddie's cart in the shed and they looked through the kitchen window and saw that the kitchen was very neat, but there was a dirty cup and saucer on the draining board by the sink.

"It shows he went off suddenly," Janet explained. "He was very tidy and he'd never have left it there." She showed them Laddie's tack hanging up in a shed, the key of which was under half a brick round at the back. Mr. Timms never took the key out with him because he'd once lost it through having a hole in his coat pocket. The tack was beautifully polished and the brass on the collar and driving pad was still bright.

Then they walked back to Deneway. Colin said, as they got near, "Let's start sleuthing tomorrow.

We could ride over here and start to track him."

"We'll bring our tea," said Susan.

"I'll bring my knife," Paul said. "Just in case one of them picks up a stone."

"Super!" Janet said. "It would be deadly dull to sleuth all by myself. I can bike with you."

"We can take it in turns to ride," Susan said.

"Oh thanks. I'm longing to see Gallant," Janet said. Gallant was Susan's pony, and Janet had seen a snapshot of him which Susan had had at school, and of course she had heard a lot about him. "I wish I could have a pony," she said, "but we've nowhere to keep one. Sleuthing's going to be fun."

"We'll be Mounted Detectives," said Paul.

"Pony Sleuths," suggested Colin. "It's going to be jolly difficult to make a start. I can't see how we're going to begin tracing him without any clues."

"Ride round and ask people if they've seen a stray pony," Susan said hopefully.

"If he did go through that place in the fence, and it didn't really look as if he did, then he'd have gone up the lane and along the path," Janet said thoughtfully.

"Where's the path?" Colin asked.

"It's just a rough sort of track that starts when the lane fizzles out at the cottage. It comes out on a common," Janet told them.

"That's the place to look," said Colin. "Why, he might be grazing there all the time."

"There's nobody living quite near there who'd find him," Janet said, "only sometimes gypsies came there. I've seen a caravan there several times. Oh golly, I hope there aren't any there now. They might have got him."

"I knew gypsies had stolen him," said Paul.

"They haven't, at least we don't know," Susan said, "so don't make things up, Paul."

But Janet felt rather anxious at the thought of gypsies finding Laddie. She had read somewhere that they could disguise a horse so that his owner wouldn't know him. What chance would they have of finding Laddie then? Or of getting him from them if they did find him?

The Fentons went home, after arranging to call for Janet the next afternoon directly after lunch. Janet played with Goloshes, who was feeling skittish and was very fierce with a cotton reel on a piece of string. But Janet kept thinking about Laddie. How difficult it was going to be to track him and how awful if Mr. Timms came home before they had found him.

Janet looked enviously at the Fentons' mounts when they arrived at Deneway early the next afternoon. "What super ponies! You are lucky!" Colin was riding a black pony of about thirteen hands two, Susan was on a bright bay and Paul was on a little red roan. "Gallant's simply lovely." Janet patted Susan's bay. "What are the others called?"

Susan pointed to Colin's black. "Midnight. Paul's is Tom Thumb. Only we generally call him Tommy."

"But we put Tom Thumb when we enter him for a show or anything, because it looks posher when it's printed in the programme," Paul said.

Janet stroked the little roan's nose. "Do you go to many shows?"

"Not very many," Susan answered. "They're not really good enough to show, but we love gymkhanas. Only Daddy jibs at our going to ones too far away as boxing's so expensive."

"Tommy's jolly good at bending races," said Paul.

"We ought to get weaving, we've no time to spare," Colin said impatiently.

"I'm ready. My tea's in my bike basket." Janet wheeled her bicycle out through the gate and called good-bye to her mother who was looking out of a window.

Susan dismounted. "You ride Gallant. I'll bike."

"Thanks awfully. I'd love to." Janet, who was wearing her jeans, mounted and Susan took her bicycle.

"Where are we going?" asked Paul.

"I think we ought to go down the lane past Mr.

Timms' cottage and along the path to the common. That's the most likely way for Laddie to have gone if he did get out."

"I hope we see some gypsies," said Paul. "I bet he's been pinched by some. Gosh, it'd be smashing if we found him and had a fight with them!"

"It'd be horrid," contradicted Susan. "We'd get hurt and they'd win. It wouldn't be a bit like fights in books or on the telly when the right people win and don't get hurt."

Janet wasn't listening or she would have agreed with Susan. She was enjoying riding Gallant, and as he was new to her she was paying careful attention so as to get to know him. He had a light mouth and carried his head well, he went into his bridle and responded to the aids when she made him trot. "He's a super pony, Sue!"

"Yes, isn't he?" Susan answered in a pleased voice. "He's keen enough to be fun but he never hots up and he jumps quite well. I think he's absolutely perfect."

"So's Tommy," Paul said at once.

"Oh yes, Tommy's a poppet! We've had him for ages," Susan told Janet. "He was Colin's first and then mine."

"If only we had a field so that I could have a pony," Janet sighed.

"If only one of them would get a stone in his hoof," grumbled Paul.

They turned up the lane and trotted past Laddie's empty field. When they came to the green, grassy path they cantered in single file, leaving Susan toiling slowly on Janet's bicycle. They had a short gallop across the common and then pulled up and waited for Susan who came bumping and wobbling across the rough grass.

"Gallant went absolutely superbly. I'm awfully sorry you had to bike," Janet told her.

"I don't mind. Where do we go now?" Susan asked.

"No gypsies," remarked Paul.

Janet looked round. She had had a secret hope that they might find Laddie grazing on the common. A road ran along beside it and she pointed. "If Laddie came here he'd have gone down there I should think. Let's try that way."

"I want to jump this gorse bush," Paul said.

So they all jumped some of the low, thick furze bushes until Paul fell off into the prickles. When he had sucked his scratched hands and caught Tom Thumb he said, "Gorse is rotten stuff, let's go on with our sleuthing."

"I'll bike, Sue," Janet said. "It's your turn to ride." But Susan said she didn't mind so Janet rode on. They went a short way along the road, which was a quiet country one, and they came to a place where it forked. "Which way now?" Colin asked.

Janet said doubtfully. "Laddie might have gone either way. Why not start our inquiries by asking at that cottage?" She pointed to a small, old-fashioned cottage at the fork in the road. She looked at Colin. "Who'll ask?"

"I don't mind." He got off Midnight. "You'd better come too as you know Laddie."

They gave their reins to Susan and Paul to hold and went up a little path to the cottage door. Colin knocked and it was opened by a short, plump, cheerful-looking woman.

"We're sorry to bother you," Colin said, "but we're trying to trace a pony that's got lost. I suppose you haven't seen or heard of one that's strayed?"

"A chestnut," said Janet, adding, "You see, we think he may have come along here."

The woman shook her head and eyed them curiously. "Where would you be from?"

"Near Trewsbury. The pony belongs to Mr. Timms and he draws the vegetable cart. I daresay you've seen him?"

"Oh yes, he comes here regular, every Tuesday. I buy fruit off him for the kiddies. Has he lost his pony?"

"He's ill and his pony's missing," Janet explained. "We think he might have strayed off across the common. I suppose you don't remember seeing a chestnut pony?"

The woman frowned. "I've not seen no pony," she said slowly, "but I woke up, several nights back it was, when a horse neighed somewhere near by. Ever so funny it sounded at night."

"When?" Colin and Janet asked together.

"I couldn't say reely," the woman answered vaguely. "Several nights ago."

"Thanks a lot. It's a terrific help. You couldn't say which road he went along?" asked Colin.

She shook her head. "I didn't hear nothing, save the neighing." They thanked her and went back to the others.

"We've got a clue," Colin said, taking Midnight's reins from Susan. "A pony came along here in the night, several nights ago; she heard him neigh."

"Gosh, in the night!" Paul said. "Horse thieves! I bet it was gypsies."

"Much more likely he just got out and strayed off," said Susan. "And it may not've been Laddie."

"We must follow up clues," said Colin. "Where do these roads go to, Jan?"

"The right-hand one comes out on the main road fairly soon. I hope he didn't go down it but if he had someone would've found him by now, and told the police probably. The other goes to a village called Sanford. Let's try it."

"Fair enough," said Colin, and turned Midnight towards the left-hand road.

"You ride now, Sue," Janet said. "My turn to bike."

"Have a go on Midnight," Colin offered, and Janet accepted with delight.

Midnight was a more difficult pony to ride than Gallant. His mouth was light and the least touch on it seemed to fret him; you needed to ride him using the aids and your legs, Janet decided. When they came to a wide strip of grass beside the road they cantered along it and Midnight began to pull. Janet let him take the lead and he settled down, but he didn't want to pull up when they reached the end. "He's keener than Gallant," she said as they waited for Colin to catch up on the bicycle.

"He gets a bit hot," Susan agreed. "He's very fast and an awfully good jumper but he's not such a nice ride as my darling Gallant." Sue patted her pony. "What about tea?"

"I'm starving," Paul said. They tied the ponies to two gates, having loosened their girths, and sat in the shade, opening their packets of provisions. They put everything in a pile and divided it into four. "They look like dogs' dinners, all muddled up," Paul said. "Would you like to ride Tommy next, Janet?"

"I'd love to. If I'm not too big for him?"

"Oh no, he's very strong and you look quite light," said Susan. "We're not going far or fast."

After tea they tidied up their picnic remains and put the papers in their haversacks to take home. Then they got on the ponies. The saddle of the bicycle had to be put down for Paul, but Janet had a quite new set of spanners and Colin did it quickly.

"The village is only a short way from here," Janet said, "and there's a blacksmith there. He'd be a good person to ask. He must see all the local ponies."

The forge stood back from the road. Colin and Paul went in to make inquiries and the girls waited outside.

"No go," Colin said when they came back. "Only he says there's a man in this village who does a bit of horse-dealing and he might be worth asking. His name's Ted Deakins."

Susan looked at her watch. "There isn't time. We ought to go home because of Paul's bedtime."

Paul scowled. "Bother my bedtime. And I don't go much earlier than you and Colin."

"You do. Hours earlier." Susan turned Gallant round.

"Are you tired of biking, Paul?" Janet asked. "As I've ridden all the time I ought to bike now. And I think your ponies are simply super."

"Tommy's best, isn't he?" Paul asked.

"I couldn't say which is best yet," she answered. It seemed the best way of dealing with a difficult question, because she liked Gallant best, so far, but she had the feeling that Midnight was probably the best pony if you were a good rider.

"Let me go on biking, I like it." Paul pedalled hard and shot ahead.

"We can't keep putting the saddle up and down," said Colin. "Shall we come over again tomorrow and see Ted Deakins? Okay for you, Jan?"

"Oh yes. We must keep at it, or Mr. Timms will come home before we find Laddie," Janet answered seriously.

"But we're on the trail," said Paul.

Would they really find Laddie, and in time for Mr. Timms' return? Janet couldn't help feeling very anxious.

CHAPTER FOUR

A SUSPICIOUS CHARACTER

"YOU must let me bike half-way at the very least. I rode all the time yesterday," Janet said when the Fentons came over to Deneway, the next afternoon.

"Oh well, we can ride any day. You start on Gallant." Susan slid off him and handed the reins to Janet.

"The same way as yesterday only further," Colin said. "We must bash on at a good pace as we were rather late home."

"We needn't waste time stopping to ask anywhere," Susan said. They trotted a good part of the way, resisted the temptation to stop and jump furze bushes on the common, and cantered on all the grassy stretches. Susan and Colin took turns to bike. They reached Sanford in good time and Colin said, "Straight through the village. The blacksmith said it's the last house. Only actually it's a bungalow. He said we couldn't miss it."

"People always say that when they tell you the way and I always do," Janet remarked.

"It's called The Haven," Colin told them. "And

this looks like the last house, or bungalow rather, so it must be it!"

"Golly! I don't call that much like a haven," Susan said disgustedly. The bungalow was very shabby; it had paint peeling off the door and the windows were very dirty. The garden was a mass of weeds, even nettles and thistles. Behind it they saw a bare-looking field with some tumble-down sheds, sad-looking hens were wandering about aimlessly and a thin goat was tethered to a stake.

"You go, Colin," Janet said.

"You jolly well come too."

"Okay then." Janet dismounted and gave Susan her reins. "We'll swap now, Sue, and I'll bike."

"Bags bike," Paul said. "And the saddle's still down low."

"I'll say it is, I kept knocking my knees on the handlebars," Susan said.

Colin and Janet went up the weedy path and Colin rapped on the door. After a short wait it was opened by an untidy-looking woman in a grubby cotton dress and bedroom slippers.

"Is Mr. Deakins at home?" Colin asked.

"Which one would you be wanting?"

"Mr. Ted Deakins," Colin replied.

"What was yer wanting 'im for?" the woman asked. She was holding the door half open as if she did not want them to see inside the bungalow.

"It's about a pony," Janet explained.

The woman looked interested. "Was yer wanting to buy one?"

"No, well, we might have to, I suppose," Colin said. "It's one that got lost. We think it strayed."

"Eh?" said the woman in a startled voice. "Strayed?" Then she stopped and looked confused.

"It's a chestnut. Has Mr. Deakins found one?" Janet asked.

"No," said the woman shortly. "He ain't got no ponies now. He 'ad to go away sudden-like, so 'e got rid of 'em."

"I suppose there wasn't a chestnut among them, one that he hadn't had long?" Colin asked.

"He did 'ave one for a few days," the woman began. Then she said crossly, "I don't know nothing about it. Why d'ye come asking questions?"

"We were told he bought and sold ponies, so we thought he might have heard of one being found," Janet explained. "I'm sorry we bothered you."

They walked back to the ponies and Janet said, "Not much good." Colin did not answer. He took Midnight's rein from Susan and stood for a moment, frowning. Then he said, "Come on. Let's do a bunk from here."

"That woman's watching us, peeping out of a

window behind a curtain," Paul announced. "I'm biking. Here, Janet, you ride Tommy."

"Come on," Colin said impatiently. He swung himself on to Midnight and jogged on, feeling for his stirrup irons as he went.

"What's up?" Susan asked, trotting alongside Midnight.

"I think that whole set-up is phoney. I'm sure that woman knows something. When we said a stray pony she nearly said something and then stopped and shut up like a clam."

"And she said he did have one for only a few days," Janet remembered.

"Is she a crook?" Paul called from where he was bicycling behind them.

"Shut up, you clot," said Colin. "I don't suppose so, but Ted Deakins might be. If so, she knows about it."

"I think he found Laddie straying and pinched him," said Janet.

Colin nodded. "Could be. So he's sold him. That's difficult."

"Terribly difficult," agreed Susan. "He might be miles away. And if he's sold we couldn't make the new owner give him up if we did find him. They wouldn't have known he was stolen."

"Is taking a straying pony stealing it?" asked Paul.

"Of course," Susan answered. "You'd know it

must belong to someone. It's not as bad as planning to steal but it's just as dishonest. And a jolly mean thing to do."

"He'd have advertised Laddie probably," Colin said thoughtfully. "That's the most likely way to sell a pony. It can't be long ago and probably in the local paper. We could look in old ones and find the advertisement."

"But we wouldn't know who'd bought him," Susan pointed out.

"No. It wouldn't help. Blast! It looks as if we've had it," Colin said despondently.

"Oh no. We can't give up," Janet cried. "Poor Mr. Timms coming back and finding Laddie gone! He'd be most frightfully sad, and what will he do about his vegetable round?"

"I don't see what we can do," said Susan. "Though it is rotten for Mr. Timms."

"This is a full stop," Colin said, "if Ted Deakins took Laddie home and sold him."

"Isn't there *any* way . . ." Janet began, touching Tom Thumb with her heel to make him keep up with the bigger ponies. "I know! Advertise."

"Gosh, yes! Why didn't we think of that before?" Colin exclaimed. "Good for you, Jan."

"What'll we say?" asked Susan. "Lost, a pony. Reward offered and all that?"

"Yes, a reward. I wonder how much we ought

to put? And how much we could raise? The advert'll cost a few bob," Colin said.

"You mustn't pay anything," Janet said quickly. "You don't even know Mr. Timms. I'll pay. And I'm sure Mummy would give something towards it."

"I'll give something. I'd like to," said Susan.

"Sue's always a push-over for a hard luck story! She's got the kindest heart in our family," Colin said laughing. "But we'll all fork out something."

"You mustn't," Janet repeated. "I don't see why you should."

"Pony Sleuths Limited! We'll go shares with everything," Sue said.

"When does the local paper come out, Jan?" Colin asked.

"The *Weekly News* comes out on Fridays. When my rabbit had young ones I advertised them in it and they all sold."

"Have you got a rabbit?" Paul asked.

"She died. When I was at school. We think it was old age. She was sweet."

"We'll send our advertisement in today. They'll take several days to print it."

"We've got a local paper at home so we could see what it says and the price of advertising," said Janet. "Let's go home and write it out."

"And we can post it on our way back to Trewsbury," Colin said. "It's a jolly bright idea. We ought to offer a reward for anyone who gives us information about a pony found straying, and also put in something to say he may have been sold lately. We can't say Ted Deakins' name or he might cut up rough—it'd be libel or something—so it's going to be difficult."

"When are we having tea?" called Paul, who was bicycling ahead of them.

"When we get home. If we have it in the garden we can make up our advertisement at the same time," Janet suggested. "And we've some shade for the ponies to stand in. But not much grass for them to eat. I don't think Daddy would like it if they went on the lawn."

"They stuff themselves pretty well all the time except when they're being ridden, so it won't hurt them," Colin said.

"It's your turn to ride, Paul," Janet shouted.

"I'm okay. I like biking. Your bike's super." Paul leaned over the handlebars and pedalled as hard as he could.

"Come on. Let's hurry and get our advert made up." Colin touched Midnight with his heels and they set off at a brisk trot.

"Oh goodness! It's difficult," Susan said a little later. "It's as bad as those beastly parsing exercises we had last term." They were sprawling on the lawn in Deneway garden. Their picnic things were spread out all round them and the ponies were tied to the fence under a tree. Susan had just torn up their fourth attempt at an advertisement.

"I wish it wasn't so horribly dear. Twenty words for six bob, it doesn't give you a chance to say anything," complained Janet.

"And it's darned hard to get what you want to say into a few words and still keep it clear what you mean," said Colin. "Let's have another stab at it. Lost. Chestnut pony about twelve hands——"

"Need we say his size? It'd save two words if we don't." Susan sucked her pencil.

"Okay." Colin began again. "Lost, full stop. Chestnut pony, full stop. Probably strayed about July fourteenth from near Trewsbury. Reward offered for information. How many's that, Sue?"

"Five more. Jan's name and address will use them up."

"If we just put the phone number that's only two," Janet said. "I'll stay at home to answer it."

"It's not very clear," Colin said, after reading it. "And it doesn't say anything about somebody possibly having bought him."

"What can we do if they have?" asked Paul. "Buy him back again?"

They looked at each other. "I was wondering about that," Janet confessed. "I've hardly any left in my post office savings. I used it to buy my bike."

"We haven't got much," Colin said. "We all

paid a bit towards our ponies, they were very expensive especially Midnight, and Daddy made up the rest. So we're pretty low."

"We could all give a little, but it probably wouldn't be enough," said Sue.

"It's extremely decent of you," Janet said. "But you mustn't. Mr. Timms is my friend, you don't even know him."

"The thing is to *find* Laddie," Colin said, "and settle about buying when it happens. If we don't finish this advert we'll miss the post. We really ought to put that thing about 'information leading to the recovery of the pony'. Advertisements always have that to stop people making something up and claiming a reward."

"Awful lot of words though," said Susan. "What about 'useful information' instead?"

After several more attempts they produced an advertisement which Colin said would do. "It's as good as we'll manage in twenty words." He read it out.

> Lost. Chestnut pony. Strayed about July 14. Trewsbury district. Possibly stolen and sold. Suitable reward for useful information.

"Phone number two words that just does it."

"Genuine information's better than useful," Susan said.

"It is rather good," Colin agreed. "You write it

out, Sue, your writing's best, and we'll get a postal order and send it off on the way home." He helped himself to a biscuit. "Is there any more orangeade?"

"Heaps." Susan passed the bottle to him. "You'll have to sit on the phone all Friday, Jan."

"I hope we don't get an awful lot of people all expecting rewards," Janet said anxiously.

CHAPTER FIVE

SLEUTHS IN ACTION

"NOT a sausage!" said Janet.

"Nothing?" asked Susan.

"Not one?" Colin's tone was unbelieving.

"Not a thing," Janet repeated. "Not a single telephone call all day and I hardly left the beastly thing in case it rang."

It was Saturday and the Fentons, who had been unable to come over on Friday because they had gone out with their mother, had ridden over to ask what answers there had been to their advertisement.

"What a sell!" said Paul. "And six bob wasted."

"Our last hope gone," Colin said. "I don't see how we can hope to trace him. We aren't terribly good sleuths."

"I simply can't bear to think of Mr. Timms coming home and finding Laddie's lost," Janet said miserably. "Specially as he asked me to look after him."

"He was lost before you began," Sue said. "You couldn't help it."

"If only I'd gone to see him the evening I came home from school! I was going to and then I met Daddy and turned back. We would have had more idea when he went, if I'd seen him then."

There was silence for a minute. Then Colin said, "Oh well. We've done our best."

"I know. But it doesn't make it any better for Mr. Timms," Janet said.

"Poor Mr. Timms!" Susan said. "But I don't see what we can do."

They were going to give up sleuthing and trying to trace Laddie, Janet thought, and her heart sank. She'd never manage it on her own. But she couldn't give up. It was different for the Fentons as they didn't know Mr. Timms. Janet remembered how fond he was of Laddie and how cheerful he always was. It was horrid to think how miserable he would be when he knew that Laddie was lost. And how could he earn his living? She couldn't give up looking for Laddie—but she couldn't think how to go on.

"We're putting up some jumps in our paddock," Colin said. "Come and try them."

"Mummy said we could ask you to tea," Susan suddenly remembered. "Come early and we can jump before tea and after."

"I'd love to. Thanks awfully. Tell me how to find your house."

Colin gave Janet directions and even drew a map

on the back of an old envelope. It looked very difficult to understand, so she wasn't sorry when she lost it.

After the Fentons had gone home Janet stayed in the garden, keeping within earshot of the telephone just in case anyone rang up with information. Someone who'd only just seen the advertisement perhaps, or just heard of a pony that had been found. But the bell only rang once and then it was someone wanting to speak to Mrs. Craig.

Advertising was no use. Janet pondered over the problem as she made her bed and dusted her room, helped with the washing up or sat in the sun with Goloshes purring on her lap. She couldn't give up thinking about it and worrying about Mr. Timms' unhappiness when he found Laddie was gone. Had Ted Deakins found Laddie? They ought to have asked lots more questions instead of being put off by the woman at The Haven. Another visit there was what was needed.

Janet said this as soon as she saw the Fentons the next day. She had bicycled over and found their house quite easily. It was on the edge of Trewsbury and was called Fairfield. There was a short drive leading up to the house which was old-fashioned, built of red brick, three storeys high and with tall windows which pushed up or down to open. At the back there were some stables and a garage. The garden was overgrown with big shrubs and a lot of trees. At the side of the house was the paddock. There were three jumps which looked very home-made and the ponies were grazing round them.

"I thought that too," Susan said. "Laddie could have been there all the time, round at the back in one of those sheds."

"Shall we go over and do some sleuthing?" Paul asked.

"It takes so long," Colin objected. "And we may not find out anything. We shan't have much time to jump." He looked across the paddock at the jumps. One of them was leaning over in a lop-sided way. "Bother! I believe the ponies have been rubbing against them and pushing them over. They're not all that strong."

"As long as you didn't drop any nails for them to eat," Susan said rather anxiously.

"Don't be a fuss-pot, Sue. Ponies are too sensible to eat nails. Come on, then, let's go and find some clues."

"It would be rather feeble to give up now we've tracked Laddie to The Haven," Janet said as they fetched the tack.

"*If* it was Laddie that woman heard in the night and *if* Ted Deakins did find him. A lot of ifs," Colin remarked.

The ponies were all easy to catch and in a very short time they were on their way to Sanford.

"Now what?" asked Paul when The Haven came in sight.

"Stop!" Colin ordered. "We don't want Mrs. Deakins to see us. We don't know that Deakins went away, she could have been telling a lie to put us off, so he could be somewhere around." Colin dismounted. "If you'll stay here with the ponies I'll scout round."

"Let me come," Paul pleaded.

"Me," said Janet. "Sorry, Paul, but I know Laddie and none of you could tell if it was him."

"If he's here what do we do? Come at night and steal him?" Paul asked.

"Certainly not," Susan said.

"We'll work that one out when we've found him," Colin said. "Coming, Jan?" They went down the road towards The Haven leaving Sue and Paul holding the ponies. They walked in single file on the grass at the side of the road and they did not talk. Because the hedge round the garden was high and overgrown, they could not be seen from the bungalow except when they passed the gate. To do this they crossed to the far side of the road and stooped down. Janet had a quick look at the bungalow and thought it looked a horrid place. But there was no one about. "What are we going to do?" she whispered.

"Snoop round in the field at the back," Colin replied. "We'll have to be careful not to be seen.

If Deakins really is a horse thief he would be awfully angry if he caught us."

Just beyond the bungalow garden there was a gate into the field which stretched right round to the back of The Haven and a good way on beyond it. It was quite a large field and there were some sheds and hen-houses dotted about in a haphazard way. Some hens were scratching in the grass and three white ducks lay asleep with their heads folded on to their backs. A goat was tethered to a stake and it bleated when it saw them at the gate. There were no ponies.

"He could be in one of those sheds." Colin nodded towards the wooden huts. "We've got to see inside them."

"All right." Janet climbed the gate and Colin vaulted it. There were five sheds, not counting hen-houses, and Colin said, "You do these near ones and I'll do the further ones." He hurried towards them, looking at the bungalow as he went.

Janet reached the first shed. The door was fastened with a hook. She opened it and looked in. Just a store-shed with sacks of something, a wheel-barrow and a heap of firewood. Not at all tidy. She shut the door and started towards the next shed. Colin, she noticed, was looking through the window of a large hut made of corrugated tin. Suddenly a pony neighed. It was quite close but Janet could not decide which shed the neigh came from and then a dog began to bark furiously. She saw a big black-and-white sheep dog by a gate which led into the field from the bungalow's garden. He was pulling at his chain which was fastened to a kennel.

Thank goodness he's chained up! Janet thought. She glanced round at Colin and saw that he was standing behind a shed and signalling frantically to her, waving her back and pointing towards The Haven. Startled, Janet took a quick look and saw that Mrs. Deakins was coming towards the garden gate and she darted behind the store-shed. Had she been seen? The dog was baying fiercely.

They waited. They could see each other and Janet watched while Colin peeped round the side of his hut. He drew back and shook his head, evidently Mrs. Deakins was still there. It seemed quite a long time before the dog was quiet. Then Colin reconnoitred and signalled to Janet to go on. Hurry, she thought, and get away quickly. This could be dangerous. She left the shelter of the store-shed and went towards the next one but as soon as they appeared in the open the dog began to bark again, straining at his chain and looking horribly savage.

Janet ran to the nearest shed and found it had only three sides and housed a broken-down cart. That hadn't taken long. Now for the next. But Colin had taken cover behind a hen-house and

Janet saw Mrs. Deakins coming to the garden gate again. She slipped back behind the cart-shed nd they waited again while Mrs. Deakins stood looking across the field and the dog barked and the goat bleated. At last the dog quietened down and Mrs. Deakins went back indoors. There were two sheds still unsearched. One was too small for a pony but the other was the largest and the farthest from the road.

As soon as they started towards it the dog began barking and Colin ran across to Janet. "Scram. We'll never do any good here."

"I'm sure he's in that big shed; he neighed," Janet said. But Colin made off towards the gate into the road and Janet followed him. They scrambled over it and dodged behind the hedge. Colin looked back, peering through the leaves. "She's there. Looking very cross. I don't think she saw us or she'd have yelled at us."

"We must look in that shed. I'm sure he's there," said Janet.

"We can't with Mrs. Deakins popping in and out," Colin answered. "There's a pony there all right and they're probably keeping him in so nobody sees him because he's not theirs."

They rejoined the others who were bored with waiting and they told them all about it. Susan said, "We simply must see if it is Laddie."

"Of course it is," Janet declared. "But we've got

to make sure. Only it's hopeless, with that dog barking as soon as he sees us and Mrs. Deakins rushing out."

"If she sees us snooping she'll know we're after Laddie and they'll hide him somewhere else before we can come with the police," said Colin.

"Is that what we're going to do?" Paul asked. "The Cops? Gosh!"

"We'll tell Daddy. He'll know what to do," said Colin. "But we must be sure Laddie's here and Mrs. Deakins mustn't see us."

"How?" Janet asked. "That dog's a brute."

Colin was frowning the way he did when he was thinking hard and Janet thought, he's got a plan. Then he said, "Somehow we must keep her busy while we get a squint at the pony in the shed."

"Bung a stone through a window!" Paul suggested. "Or ring the bell and run away!"

"Certainly not, nothing like that," Susan said severely.

"Of course not, you clot," Colin said. "Jan and I were the ones who went and asked her about a stray pony so she knows us. Did she see you and Paul, do you think, Sue?"

"Not properly. We stayed in the road."

"I saw her peeping at us through the window so she must have seen me," Paul said.

"Then Sue must do it," said Colin.

"What?" Susan asked, rather anxiously.

"Go to the door and get her talking. Keep her there while we rush up the field and look in the shed. Jan must come as she knows Laddie," Colin explained, "otherwise I could do it alone."

"Oh!" Susan said blankly. "What can I talk about?"

"Something that really interests her," said Janet. "Not just asking the way somewhere. I know, say you want to buy a pony and you've heard Mr. Deakins sells them. She got interested when we said we wanted a pony. I bet she'd be keen on making some money."

"She'll be suspicious if she does recognize me," Susan objected.

"It doesn't matter, as long as you keep her talking at the front door," Colin said. "Say you've lost your pony and want to buy another, then it won't matter if she does know you again. Ask if Mr. Deakins could get you one. Say anything, but keep her at the door as long as possible."

"It's going to be awfully difficult," Susan said. "Can you manage three ponies, Paul? We'll tie Tommy to something so you've only two to hold."

"They'll stand without holding. Better be ready to scram if we have to in a hurry. Anything might happen," Colin said and Janet wondered if it would be dangerous. Suppose that dog got loose? Or Ted Deakins appeared suddenly and was angry? But they had to risk it to find Laddie.

Susan said, "You get round to the field and hurry. I may not be able to keep her talking for long. I'll never think of enough to say."

Janet and Colin watched her go up the path to the front door. Then they dashed along to the field gate. Colin vaulted it and Janet climbed over. The dog began to bark and to rattle his chain as he sprang and tugged.

They reached the shed. It was a large wooden building with a stable half-door which was fastened with a piece of string. It took a minute or two to untie and while Colin undid it they could hear a pony stamping inside and a smell of stable hung round them. Janet's heart was beating fast—was this the end of the search? Colin swung open the top door and they looked in eagerly. Two ponies were standing together. A brown and a skewbald. No chestnut. "He's not there," Janet said. She was painfully disappointed.

"Come on back," Colin said. "Hurry, Sue may have run out of things to talk about."

The dog was still barking and rattling his chain as they ran back towards the gate into the road. Then suddenly he was quiet. It was not until they heard his chain clinking quite near them that they realized he was loose and pursuing them silently. Janet's heart seemed to come up into her throat and Colin yelled "Run!" They were already running fast but fear made them find some extra speed and they raced towards the gate. That horrible dog! Janet thought she could feel him at her heels. Colin said, "Go on, Jan!" and hung back while she hurled herself over the gate before he vaulted it. They tore down the road. The gate wouldn't stop him, Janet thought, as she made for her bicycle which was propped against the fence.

"Get on. Buck up," Colin shouted and Susan, who was already there, mounted Gallant quickly. Paul was on Tom Thumb and Colin jumped on Midnight as Janet pushed her bicycle on to the road. Quicker to get on than a pony, she thought, but that big dog could run as fast as she could bike. He had begun barking again so she looked back. He had come through the gate but his chain was caught in it.

"He can't follow. He's stuck by his chain," she said, with great relief.

All the same they hurried for quite a long way.

"What happened?" Paul asked when they slowed down to a walk. "Is Laddie there?"

"No," Janet answered. "Two ponies, but not Laddie. It's sickening. I was sure he was there."

"So was I," Susan said, disappointedly. "I'm sorry I couldn't keep her talking longer. It began all right, but when the dog kept barking she said something about kids hanging round and upsetting the dog and she rushed off."

"His chain must have bust," said Colin. "We

were lucky to get away. He sounded awfully fierce."

"I was terrified. I didn't know I could run so fast," Janet said. "All for nothing; we're back where we began."

"I found some clues while I was waiting," Paul announced importantly. "I made a search and found these." He produced an old bus ticket and a cigarette end from his pocket. "They were down by the gate of The Haven."

"Fancy picking up those dirty things!" Susan said.

"They're *clues*!" Paul insisted. "It's rained three days ago and they're not spoilt so that shows they're fresh."

Colin took them and examined them. "I can't see that they tell us anything. A cigarette end's the corniest old clue! A bus ticket from Tillmouth. That is a bit odd if Deakins used it because he'd take a return."

"Perhaps it wasn't him," said Susan.

"Was the cigarette end with it, Paul?" Colin asked.

"Yes, close to it."

"Does Mrs. Deakins use lipstick?" Colin asked next.

"Yes. An orange one. Horrid!" Susan replied.

"Then this cigarette wasn't hers or the lipstick would 've come off," Colin said. "So it's probably

Deakins' and he had the bus ticket too and threw them away together when he got home."

"Are my clues important?" Paul inquired.

"Could be," Colin answered slowly. "If he only had a ticket back from Tillmouth how did he go in?"

"How?" Susan asked puzzled. "I don't see——"

"If he took a pony," Colin said, "he'd come back by bus. He could have taken Laddie to Tillmouth and sold him there."

CHAPTER SIX

ANOTHER CLUE

BUT when they thought it over, as they trotted back towards Deneway, even Colin failed to see how Paul's clues could be any help in tracing Laddie. Tillmouth was a large seaside town about nine miles away. They couldn't search it for a chestnut pony, especially as the bus ticket was such a slender clue that it might not have anything to do with Laddie's disappearance.

"We really are at a dead end," Colin said. "Sorry, Jan, but it's no go."

"Come over and see us tomorrow, in case we've thought of something," Sue said, seeing that Janet was looking very depressed.

"Okay. I'll come in the afternoon. I'm riding at Miss Parry's in the morning. I'm having a lesson once a week these hols. She has awfully good ponies. Melody, her best one, has won lots of prizes. I'd simply adore to ride him at a Show but I don't know if I'll ever be good enough. I generally ride Starlight. He's a grey and he's the most gorgeous pony. I thought I'd ask Miss Parry the best way to find a lost pony."

"Good idea," Susan said. "Come and tell us what she says."

Then they reached Deneway and Janet dismounted from Midnight. She patted his neck and laid her cheek against it for a minute. He was so warm and silky and he smelt so nice! Lucky Fentons to have ponies, but she was lucky too to go riding with them every day. Only Laddie being lost spoiled everything. However could she tell Mr. Timms?

The next morning Mrs. Craig drove Janet to the Riding School and left her there while she went into Trewsbury to do some shopping. Janet rode Starlight and Miss Parry said, at the end of her lesson, that she was improving.

"Shall I be good enough to ride Melody?" Janet asked.

"If you go on like this, I think you could ride him before the end of the holidays. We'll see how he goes for you and if you get on all right with him you could ride him in one of the small Shows."

"Oh, how marvellous!" Janet's face went pink with pleasure. "I say, Miss Parry, how would you find a pony that was lost?" And she told her about Mr. Timms and Laddie.

"If advertising was no use I don't know what you can do," Miss Parry said. "I expect he got out through that weak patch that you found in the fence. Ponies are very clever at that, specially if they're alone in a field. If he strayed somebody's bound to find him sooner or later. They'd most likely report it to the police. Unless it was someone dishonest who kept him and said nothing about it."

"That's what I'm afraid of," Janet sighed.

"He could have got into a field with some other horses," Miss Parry said, "and not been noticed yet. Horses and ponies are very sociable and they like each other's company. Laddie might well have found some others in a field and joined them. If they were turned out for the summer the owner may not see them every day, though of course he ought to, so Laddie wouldn't be found at once."

"Then he might tell the police who'd ring up Daddy," said Janet. It did seem a likely solution to the mystery.

"I shouldn't give up hope," Miss Parry said.

As long as Mr. Timms didn't come home yet, Janet thought, it was horrid not to want him to be well again but he'd be so upset if he came back and found Laddie was missing. And they couldn't go and see him in hospital again, she thought sadly, because if they did she'd have to mention Laddie.

"Cheer up," said Miss Parry, seeing her looking grave and thoughtful. "He may turn up any day."

Then Mrs. Craig came to collect Janet and as they drove home she told her mother about her riding and how she was going to be allowed to ride Melody soon.

"Is that one of Miss Parry's best ponies?" Mrs. Craig asked. She was always slightly vague about ponies.

"Oh, Mummy, you must remember Melody. He won First at the Show we went to in the Easter hols. Sandra Thompson rode him. It'll be simply marvellous to ride him in a Show. Can I go over to the Fentons' this afternoon?"

Mrs. Craig said, "Yes, if you're sure they want you again. You've seen them almost every day. Don't overdo it, darling."

"Sue *asked* me to come," replied Janet. "It's simply smashing them being so near. I can bike there in a quarter of an hour. The boys are nearly as nice as Sue, and they're awfully decent and unselfish about letting me have lots of turns riding."

She found Susan alone when she went over to Fairfield in the afternoon. "The boys have gone to the river," Sue explained. "Colin heard that there's a swimming pool there and he's awfully keen about swimming, so they rushed off. Paul has just learnt to swim and he's keen too."

"Have they given up sleuthing?" Janet asked.

"Colin thinks we're stuck. So it's a waste of time when he might be swimming. He says we'll never do any good now."

"Do you think so?" asked Janet.

Susan frowned thoughtfully. Then she said, "I don't honestly think we're likely to find Laddie, but I think it's worth going on trying because of Mr. Timms. And you never know, we might find him."

"I think so too," Janet said. She told Susan what Miss Parry had said. "She thinks he may turn up in time. But I hate waiting. And the awful thing is that Mr. Timms may come home soon."

"I know. I keep thinking about it," Susan said sympathetically. "It's so awfully sad for him."

"I'm going to ride Melody at a Show, if my riding goes on improving," Janet told her, "and of course I'm going to improve! He's a smashing pony."

"Oh, that'll be terrific!" Susan said. "And we might go to the same Show too, that'd be fun. I say, Jan, there's a Gymkhana next Saturday and Daddy says we may go to it and have a horse-box, as it's not far away. Could you come? There'll be heaps of room in the horse-box for us all. We can all squash into the little compartment at the back. It's super fun."

"I'd adore to," Janet said.

"And you could ride Gallant in one of the races. Midnight's a bit of a handful as he hots up rather, Colin manages him better than any of us, but you could ride Tommy in something. He's awfully good because he's so sensible and never gets excited. He's easy to get on and off quickly too, as he's small."

"Thanks most awfully," Janet said fervently. "I'd simply love to. Only I've never ridden in a gymkhana so I'd probably muck it up. I'm sure I wouldn't be any good."

"Not to worry. We hardly ever win anything but it's terrific fun," Susan said. "And it's only a small gymkhana. You don't have to enter beforehand. We can decide what we are all going in for when we get there."

"It'll be smashing!" Janet said. "I've always longed to ride at one. There are so many people wanting Miss Parry's ponies for gymkhanas that she gets booked up ages before."

"Shall we practise?" Susan suggested.

"Oh yes, let's," Janet said happily.

They stuck some sticks in the ground and made a course for a Bending Race. Janet rode Tommy first and she found that he was very good at it. He knew all about it and he was very quick at turning round the end pole. Then they changed ponies and Janet rode Gallant. Although he was a larger pony he was no faster than Tom Thumb for he was too sedate and disinclined to hurry.

"He wakes up a bit in a real race," Susan said, "but he never gets hotted up. And very often the slower steadier ponies win because the faster ones get too excited and knock the poles."

After practising Bending they jumped the ponies over the jump which Colin had made. Gallant jumped very carefully and smoothly and Janet enjoyed it.

Then Susan said, "I keep thinking about Mr. Timms and Laddie. We oughtn't to give up so easily. You never know but we *might* find him."

"That's just what I've been thinking." Janet smoothed Gallant's mane. "Only I don't see what we can do."

"Shall we go to Sanford again?" Susan suggested. "And ask people in the village if they saw a pony at Deakins' that was like Laddie? It really does seem as if he might have been there. If he went along past the cottage where the woman heard a pony neigh, he'd be bound to have got there."

"Unless he went the other way where the road forks by the cottage and then he'd have come out in the main road to Trewsbury," Janet said.

"If he'd done that, someone would have seen him and told the police," said Susan. "It looks as if he went to Sanford and I can't help thinking that the Deakins know something about it. It wouldn't do any harm to go back and ask about him. Not the blacksmith or that horrid Mrs. Deakins. Just anyone we meet."

"I don't suppose it'll be any good but it's worth trying," said Janet. "And it's a nice way to ride."

Susan told Mrs. Fenton where they were going

and they set off. Susan rode Midnight, saying Colin wouldn't mind, and he was faster than Tom Thumb who, being a small pony, had a slow walk and was inclined to hold them back.

On the way they talked about the Gymkhana on Saturday. Susan offered to let Janet ride Gallant in the Bending Race but Janet, though very grateful, thought Sue should ride him.

"Then ride him in something else," Sue said, "we'll see when we get there. You must have one race on him. And you could ride Tommy in the Obstacle Race. I don't expect Paul would mind. He's not very good at doing things quickly and he gets flustered. He likes Bending as he just leaves it to Tommy and once he got Third. You're fairly light and you could jump on and off Tommy quickly and he's really quite good as he's small and nippy."

"I'd love to ride him if Paul doesn't mind," Janet said. It was something she had always longed to do.

When they reached Sanford they stopped. It had seemed easy when they had thought of going back there to ask people questions but how should they begin?

"We can't bother people by going to their houses," Janet said.

"And there's no one about," Susan said looking round. "They must all be having their tea. We'll miss ours," she added. "Let's ride through the village and then come back again. If we meet anybody we can ask them."

They heard the blacksmith hammering on his anvil as they went past. It was no use asking him again so they rode on. A man went by on a cycle but they couldn't shout at him and ask him to stop. How do real detectives do it, Janet wondered? They turned before reaching The Haven as they didn't want Mrs. Deakins to see them. As they walked the ponies through the little village again Janet said, "It's much more difficult than I thought. I don't see how we can ask people when there's no one to ask."

Just as she spoke a large dog shot out of a garden gate, followed by a small boy who was yelling at him; two girls were running after them.

Gallant shied, taking Janet by surprise so that she lost both stirrups and shot forward on to his neck. He stood still, trembling slightly, and Janet managed to recover herself. She patted him and spoke to him soothingly and he stopped quivering.

Midnight had swung round, half-rearing and snorting and Sue was trying to control him. She quietened him and he stood looking round and fidgeting.

The two girls who had been chasing the small boy and the dog stopped and one of them said: "Sorry we frightened them."

"They're all right, thanks," Susan said.

The girls came up and patted Gallant. "They're sweet," they said; "what are their names?" Susan told them and asked, "Do you like ponies?"

"Yes," said the larger girl. "Specially Edna, she's crazy about horses."

The smaller girl smiled rather shyly and said, "I've always liked ponies."

"Actually," said Susan, "we're looking for a pony that's lost and we think he came this way. I suppose you haven't seen one?"

"He's chestnut," Janet said, "and a little bit smaller than these two." Gallant was thirteen hands and Midnight thirteen two.

The girls shook their heads.

"We went and asked at the Deakins' because the blacksmith told us he dealt in ponies," Janet told them, "so Mr. Deakins might have heard if one was found. But he was away and Mrs. Deakins didn't know anything about the ponies."

The two girls exchanged glances. "Those Deakins 'ud say anything," said the taller girl.

"I wouldn't put anything past Ted Deakins," agreed Edna. "And he wasn't away—just pretending he was, because he didn't know what you wanted. Guilty conscience!"

"We did wonder if he'd found Laddie, but he's not there. We looked in the sheds behind the bungalow," said Janet.

"What colour did you say?" Edna demanded suddenly.

"Chestnut."

"That's a sort of red, isn't it?"

"Yes, reddish, lighter and more fawny than this one." Janet patted Gallant's bay neck. "And his mane and tail are lighter."

"I did see a pony like that the other day," Edna told them. "A man was leading him. They came from Deakins'."

"When? Where did they go?" cried Janet and Susan.

"I couldn't say. It was about a week ago. One evening."

"Evening?" asked Janet. "Quite late?"

"Not late," replied Edna. "The bus had come in and it gets here just after five. We've only one a day here."

"Where does it come from?" Susan asked.

"Tillmouth. But it goes through Trewsbury and a lot of places before it gets here."

"Are you sure the pony was chestnut and with a light mane and tail?" Susan asked.

"Oh yes, I noticed specially as he looked so pretty," answered Edna. "It wasn't Mr. Deakins with him but a man rather like him."

"Thanks awfully. It must have been Laddie." They said good-bye and Edna said, "I hope you find him."

Then they rode home feeling rather pleased with themselves at having found out something more about Laddie's disappearance. They'd done some successful sleuthing.

"I can't see that it's much use," Colin said, when they told him. "Jolly good finding it out, but it mayn't have been Laddie and if it was, we don't know where he went."

"The man must have come from Tillmouth, as we thought from the bus ticket Paul found," Janet said.

"It's miles away. And a big place. We can't go there on the off chance of seeing Laddie," Colin protested. "Everything we've found out's so vague and without proof."

That was true, Janet knew, and yet something might lead them to Laddie. And didn't detectives have to follow up every clue until they found the right one?

"I'm going to swim every day," Colin said. "It's a smashing pool."

"Smashing," echoed Paul. "I'm going, too."

The boys were losing all interest in finding Laddie, Janet thought, sleuthing had been fun to them and now they were tired of it.

"We must practise for the Gymkhana," Susan said. "It's the first one since last hols, so we'll need lots of time to practise hard. We shan't have much time to sleuth till after Saturday."

So even Sue was giving up; you couldn't blame them as they didn't know Mr. Timms. But Janet was sure she'd never find Laddie alone. Unless she had a brainwave. And brainwaves don't always come just when you want them.

CHAPTER SEVEN

GYMKHANA

IT was very exciting helping to box the ponies. Midnight jibbed and backed away so persistently that Janet thought they'd never get him in. But the driver, whose name was Fred, took him from Colin and coaxed him up the ramp. He said he often got worse ones than that, and if a horse really jibbed at going in, the best way was for two people to clasp hands round his quarters, just above the hocks, and pull him forward.

It was fun to climb up into the compartment behind the ponies. They crowded round the window to wave to Mrs. Fenton, who was following in the car with a picnic lunch for them all, and as the horse-box moved off Janet sank down on to one of the seats and grinned at Sue who was sitting opposite to her. She had always envied the children she had seen arriving at Shows in a horse-box and now she was doing it.

There were only two seats so the boys stood leaning against the partitions dividing the ponies. The small compartment was crowded up with haynets, bundles of grooming kit and the ponies' tack.

"I hope Bending comes first, before Midnight gets too hotted up, or he'll knock the poles for six," said Colin.

"Let's go in for absolutely everything," said Susan.

The ponies travelled very quietly and were easy to unbox. Janet helped Susan take off Gallant's tail bandage and knee-boots. Then they groomed him and put on his tack. The boys had their ponies ready by then and they all went to the Secretary's Tent to make their entries.

Colin entered Midnight for Bending, the Dressing Up Race and the Polo Race. "Not for the Potato Race or the V.C. Race because he hates having to keep stopping for the potatoes and he'd be scared in the V.C."

Susan put Gallant in for everything except the Polo Race, because neither she nor Janet was any good at hitting a ball. "Would you like to ride him in the Dressing Up Race and Musical Poles, Jan?"

"I'd adore too—if you don't want to," Janet answered.

"I'll have lots of others to go in for," Sue said. "Which are you doing, Paul?"

"Bending, Potato Race, Dre ssing Up andMusical Poles. And the Obstacle Race for Jan. I'm not going in for the V.C. Race because you have to jump and it might be too high for Tommy."

"More likely too high for you, and you'd come off," Colin said.

They had an early picnic lunch with Mrs. Fenton, in the shade under some trees, with the ponies tied up close beside them. All round were other children and ponies and Janet enjoyed feeling she was one of them, instead of just watching as she usually did.

The Bending Race was the first on the programme. It was divided into two, for riders over eleven years and for those under eleven. Colin and Susan rode in the older ones' race and went in the first Heat. Midnight played up and lost valuable ground by refusing to start. Then he went very fast and was catching up when he knocked over a pole. Gallant went steadily and carefully, but turned a little wide at the end and lost ground. Sue hustled him along and just got into second place. "Bad luck you're not in the Final," Janet said.

"He went jolly well, though," replied Susan.

Paul rode Tom Thumb in the under eleven race. They watched the others critically, for Paul was in the last Heat, and decided that Tom Thumb was as good as any there.

"Just keep him going, Paul, don't fuss him," Colin said.

Paul nodded. "Tommy knows all about it."

Tom Thumb was the first away when the starter dropped his flag and he gave a faultless display of bending. He was the smallest pony in the race but he scuttled along, threading his way in and out of the poles, and not going an inch out of his way. He went so close it looked as if he was bound to touch them and Janet held her breath. Colin and Susan were unconcerned for they knew Tom Thumb. He nipped round the end pole before the others and came charging up the line of posts with Paul sitting still and keeping his feet close to his pony's sides. As they passed the last pole they were in front but, galloping to the Winning Post, larger ponies gained on them and Janet clutched Sue's arm in her excitement as Paul and Tommy held on and just won.

"Jolly good," said Colin. "Paul's had a Third on Tommy, I hope he gets First."

"Tommy's getting old so he's not very fast," Susan said. "Colin and I won Bending Races on him ages ago."

"Oh, Paul, it was exciting. You must win the Final," Janet told him. But he was beaten into second place by a larger pony and he tied the blue rosette on Tom Thumb's browband with pride.

The Potato Race came next. Susan won her Heat and then the Final, thanks to Gallant's steadiness. Paul dropped his potato and lost a lot of time in getting on again after picking it up.

Then they had the Dressing Up Race. The competitors had to ride to a line of clothing, heaped up in piles, and put on the clothes in the pile they found opposite to them, before riding back to the Winning Post. When Janet and Gallant reached the clothes Colin was already turning over his assortment of garments and trying to sort them out. Janet seized a large white thing and held it up. What on earth—? A clown's suit. Easy! She stepped in, pulled it up and slipped her arms into the sleeves. Three buttons, bright red ones, down the front were quickly done up. She rammed on the hat, which was white with a red pompom, and glanced round. Colin was trying to squeeze himself into a sailor suit. Further down the line a Red Indian was pulling on a feathered headdress and other children were struggling into various clothes. The Red Indian would be ready in a minute, Janet thought, realizing suddenly that she was first. She got her foot in her stirrup and swung herself up but she hadn't thought to turn Gallant when she got off and he was facing the wrong way. Another time she'd know. She pulled him round, dug her heels into his sides and set off at a smart canter. But the Red Indian, a boy on a dun pony, was ahead of her. He hadn't bothered to get on properly before starting and he was clinging on and pulling himself up into the saddle as the dun made for the Winning Post. Janet hurried Gallant as much as she could but they couldn't catch the dun.

"Second," Sue said. "Terrific, Jan! And your first gymkhana."

"I was terribly lucky in getting this which is easy to put on," Janet said, pulling off the clown's dress. She was very proud of winning a rosette. She'd never dared even to hope she'd win one.

Paul had no success in the under elevens'Dressing Up Race. He was unlucky in getting a very baggy Pierrot costume and he couldn't find out how to put it on.

In the V.C. Race the competitors had to dash across the ground, jumping a low hurdle, and pick up a dummy figure which was made of sacking stuffed with straw. Then they came back over the jump. Susan was one of the last to reach the dummies, but Gallant stood like a rock while she got off, lifted the figure and put it in front of the saddle, and then mounted. Other ponies were backing away from the dummies and snorting in alarm. All except the boy on the dun who was on and away in a minute. Susan followed him and a girl on a bright chestnut caught her up but when they jumped the hurdle the girl dropped her dummy. Gallant jumped carefully and smoothly and brought Susan in to win another Second. Two Blue Rosettes! and a Red one!

"Now it's the Obstacle Race," announced Paul.

A tractor drove on to the field towing a trailer laden with bales of straw. These were tipped off and the stewards arranged them in three long rows, a short distancc apart. Other stewards were hanging buns on bits of string to a long cord stretched between two poles. Beyond this stood a row of buckets. "It looks exciting," Janet said. "I wonder what we have to do?"

One of the Stewards told them. "Ride across the bales of straw, jumping them. There are three. At the end get off and come back over them leading your pony. Get on and ride across to the buns"—he pointed—"eat one without touching it with your hands. Then ride on to the buckets. There's an apple and some water in each one. You must take the apple out with your teeth." Some of the children groaned. "Got it? Quite clear?"

"Yes," they all answered.

Janet on Tom Thumb and Susan on Gallant were side by side when they lined up at the start. The boy on the dun was just beyond Gallant and Janet thought he was sure to win. She and Sue reached the straw bales together. They were a pony's length apart, like the grid she jumped at Miss Parry's. Tommy pricked his ears, stopped and smelt the straw. When Janet urged him he scrambled over it. The next two bales he jumped very slowly. Gallant was popping over them neatly and the boy on the dun was already coming back. Janet jumped off. She turned Tommy and got over the first bale. "Come on, Tommy," she urged. He jumped it, nearly knocking her down and they did the next two bales quickly. They were neck and neck with Gallant as they went to the buns. A girl on a grey caught them up and the boy on the dun was already nibbling at a bun.

Janet jumped off and began to bite at one. It was a doughnut and the sticky sugar smeared her cheeks but it swung away in a maddening manner when she tried to get hold of it with her teeth. Not too big bites seemed to be best and she worked her way through it. Then she turned round. Tommy had gone!

She looked round frantically. Sue was mounting Gallant and the dun had galloped on to the row of buckets. All round her ponies stood while children made grabs at swinging doughnuts, munched and laughed. *Why* hadn't she kept his rein looped round her wrist?

Then she saw him. A rather plump sandy-haired girl in a dark red blazer was leading him towards her. Janet rushed to meet them, grabbed the reins, shouted "Thanks" and scrambled on. She rode the short distance to the buckets without bothering about stirrups, hurled herself off and knelt in front of the nearest bucket. This time she kept hold of her reins.

The apple bobbed about. She nearly had it then —You mustn't mind getting wet at this—Tom Thumb's head came over her shoulder, she was pushed aside and his muzzle plunged into the bucket. He drew out the apple which he munched noisily. "*Tommy!*" exclaimed Janet and the onlookers laughed. She got up. Her shirt was wet all down the front and was sticking to her. At least four people had finished the race so she walked towards them to ask Sue how she had done.

She met the girl in the red blazer and stopped to say, "Thanks awfully for catching him."

The girl patted him. "He's sweet. What's his name?"

Janet told her. "Mine's Janet. What's yours?"

"Karen. Do you ride in lots of gymkhanas?"

"No, this is my first. He doesn't belong to me, he's only lent for this race. Have you got a pony?"

"No," Karen answered. "I'd simply love to have one but we've nowhere to keep one."

"Nor have we," said Janet. "Do you get much riding?"

"Only a lesson sometimes. Mummy thinks it's too dear. But I've ridden on the sands lately, most days, as there's a man who hires out donkeys and he's just got a pony too. It's a shilling and he doesn't let you go very far but it's better than nothing."

Paul came up to them saying the Musical Poles were next and could he have Tom Thumb. Janet was to ride Gallant, so she said good-bye to Karen and went with Paul.

"What happened in the Obstacle Race?" he

asked. "You seemed to be going jolly well till you got to the bob apples."

"Tommy ate the apple!"

"I ought to have warned you not to let him. As a matter of fact," Paul said, "you need sticky out teeth to be good at bob apples."

Poles had been set up in a big circle and a loud speaker was blaring out the strains of "John Peel" as they took their places. There were a lot of competitors but both Janet and Paul stayed in for quite a long while. Tom Thumb was so quick that he always managed to get to the nearest post when the music stopped. Besides, he knew all about it.

But as people dropped out and the poles got farther and farther apart, faster ponies reached them first. Paul came out and, next time, Janet found herself a long way from a post. Gallant had been going beautifully but speed wasn't his strong point and she couldn't get to the pole in time.

"He's an angel! He went superbly! Thank you most awfully for letting me ride him," Janet said to Susan. "It's been the most heavenly day I've ever had."

"A First and Three Seconds. It's the best day we've had for ages," Susan said. "It's been terrific fun."

It wasn't until she got home that Janet remembered about Laddie and it was like a cloud on her happiness.

CHAPTER EIGHT

THE CLUE OF THE RED BLAZER

"OH, Janet, I heard that Mr. Timms is coming home tomorrow," Mrs. Craig said on the Monday after the gymkhana, when they were at breakfast.

Janet put down her knife and gazed at her mother. "Oh, that's ghastly. Laddie——"

"I know," Mrs. Craig said. "I was sure he'd have turned up by now. It is rather awkward."

Mr. Craig put down his newspaper. "I'm afraid it doesn't look as if he will turn up now. The police would have heard of it if a pony had been found. I'm afraid, Janet, that your Mr. Timms has lost his pony. It's too bad, poor old chap!"

Janet's eyes filled with tears. "And he asked me to look after Laddie."

"You couldn't help it, dear, the pony had gone before then," said her mother.

"No. It's not your fault," said Mr. Craig.

"But what can we *do*?" Janet asked wildly.

"There's nothing we can do," her father said. "You and your friends have done all you can, riding round looking for him. If there was anything we *could* do, I'd be glad to help." Mr. Craig got up to go to his work.

Janet went out to see him off. Then she came back indoors to find her mother and to ask her if she could go over to the Fentons.

She found them cleaning their tack in the stables behind the house. "Mr. Timms is coming home tomorrow," she announced.

Susan said, "Oh, how dreadful! We're no nearer finding Laddie."

"Gosh, that's torn it!" Colin said. "I did hope he still might turn up somewhere. But there's no hope of anything happening by tomorrow."

"I hoped too," said Janet. "Specially after Miss Parry saying he might be in a field somewhere with other horses."

"But that man took him away from Deakins' in the evening," Susan reminded her.

Colin put down the girth he was brushing. "Evening. That's a clue. He can't have been going far, you see."

"If he came on the bus he might have been going anywhere. The girl said it went all round the place," Susan said. "So he might have got on anywhere."

"It comes from Tillmouth and my bus ticket said Tillmouth," pointed out Paul.

"It does look like Tillmouth," Colin agreed. "And he could walk back there, leading a pony.

Tillmouth's not as far from Deakins' as it is from here. Sanford's at least three miles nearer. But we can't go all the way to Tillmouth and then trail round looking for a pony."

"We could ask at Riding Stables there," suggested Susan. "There's sure to be some, as visitors like riding along the sands."

"Oh, I've thought of something," cried Janet. "That girl at the gymkhana who caught Tommy when I let him go while I was eating the dough-nut—she said she had rides on the sands. And," Janet almost shouted, "she said a man who hired out donkeys had *just got a pony*."

"It must be Laddie," said Susan excitedly.

"Where does she live? Tillmouth?" Colin asked.

"I don't know. I never asked her. Paul said the Musical Poles were starting and I left her. I never thought about it again as the gymkhana was so exciting."

"What's her name?" Susan asked. "Do you know?"

"Only Karen. She didn't say her surname. I do wish I'd thought of it then. I could've asked her everything," Janet said disconsolately. "I was a clot!"

"Let's go and find Laddie. We might swim in the sea," proposed Paul. "It must be him."

"It'd be worth having a bash at it if we were sure it was Tillmouth," Colin said. "There's several other seaside places fairly close and Karen might have come from any of them. Marlmouth's not far."

"The bus ticket was a clue to Tillmouth," said Paul.

"I wish we'd kept it," Colin said. "Marlmouth might look like Tillmouth on an old ticket which had been on the ground for several days and got grubby and rubbed out."

"The bus came from there," persisted Paul.

"It's the only bus to Sanford so the man'd have to come on it," Janet told him. "You change at Trewsbury."

"If only there was more time," sighed Sue.

"If only I'd asked Karen a bit more," said Janet. She frowned as she thought about it. Mr. Timms coming home tomorrow. But there was just a slight chance of finding Laddie.

"You don't know her other name?" Colin asked and Janet shook her head. "Her people might be in the Telephone Book," he explained.

Janet said crossly, "I told you I don't know anything, except her name's Karen and she rides a pony on the sands. One that's come to the place quite lately."

"It's not worth going to Tillmouth on the off chance," Colin said. "If we'd more time we could go to each place in turn. But we've only today so we've got to go to the right one."

"I know!" cried Janet. "Her school. She was wearing a red blazer. Dark red with a crest on the pocket. If we could find out what colours the schools wear, we'd know which town she lives in."

"Brilliant!" exclaimed Colin. "That's real detective work."

"Unless she goes away to boarding school," Susan remarked.

"She might," Janet agreed. "If none of the schools near here have red blazers, we'll know she does. How can we find out about them?"

"Don't you know anyone who goes to school in Tillmouth?" Susan asked. "Or any of the other schools near?"

Janet thought. "No. They go to Trewsbury High School from round here. I don't know anyone at Tillmouth or Marlmouth. Can't we go to Tillmouth and look?"

"If we go to the wrong place today, we've had it," said Colin. There was silence for several minutes. There didn't seem to be any way of finding out where Karen lived. Mr. Timms would come home tomorrow.

Susan said slowly, "Look, people have to buy school clothes."

"Well? So what?" Colin asked impatiently.

"Local shops," Susan explained. "They'd know which school wore red blazers."

"Gosh, that's rather bright," said Colin. "The

sort of big shop that sells practically everything besides clothes. They'd know. Can you think of one, Jan?"

"No. We hardly ever go to Tillmouth. Mummy shops in Trewsbury and when we go to the sea we go to a little tiny beach further on." How maddening it was, the way they kept coming to a stop just when they seemed to be getting somewhere. "Trewsbury shops," she said. "Some of them have branches at Tillmouth. Once Mummy wanted something and a shop got it for her from their Tillmouth branch. Mummy would know."

"So would Mummy. She's done lots of shopping in Trewsbury since we came here." Susan went to ask and Janet went on cleaning Gallant's bridle for her.

After a short time Susan came back. "Mummy can't think of the names of any shop with a Tillmouth branch. Shall we ring up your mother?"

"Oh, she'll be out. She's going shopping. Bother!" More delays. And they'd only today left.

"Paper bags," Paul said. "They have the names of shops on them and it says branches at other places."

"Golly, everyone's bright today," said Colin, "except me. Let's find some. Clothes shops, not grocers or bakers."

"Mummy bought me some shirts and they were in a big bag with the name on it," Paul said.

Susan routed in the drawer where paper was kept and pulled it out. "French Ltd. Drapers. Also at Tillmouth and Marlmouth——" she gave a whoop of triumph. "Both places. We can ask them about schools at both. In luck at last!"

They crowded round the telephone to try and hear what was said when Susan got through to French's. The voice, replying to her request, sounded far away and crackly and though Janet leaned on Susan's shoulder she could not hear the words. "Thank you so much," Susan said, when the voice stopped. She put down the receiver and said triumphantly, "Tillmouth Secondary Girls' School."

"Oh boy, we've done it!" said Colin. "Let's go."

"Now. At once," Janet urged. There wasn't a minute to lose. Suppose Laddie disappeared from the beach just before they got there!

"I'll ask Mummy if we may," Susan said.

"Oh, I must too. And she won't be home till lunch time. It'll waste ages," Janet said. "Unless I write a note and go back and leave it. And that'll waste time too."

At first Mrs. Fenton didn't want them to go so far. But when Susan explained everything, and how Mr. Timms was coming home tomorrow, she gave in. "Do you want to take sandwiches?" she asked.

"We can't wait for them," Janet said desperately.

"Need we, Mummy?" asked Susan. "We must hurry. It may take time to find the man with the donkeys."

So Mrs. Fenton gave Susan money to buy buns with—"though I don't approve of your lunching off buns, but just this once"—and she promised to ring Mrs. Craig at lunch time and tell her where they had gone and why.

They were soon on the road. Nine miles to go and Laddie at the end of it. Or so they hoped.

"I shan't believe it till I see him," Janet said, bicycling alongside Susan and Gallant.

"I'm wondering what happens when we find him," Susan answered. "Can we just grab him and bring him home? Suppose this man's bought him?"

"Once we've found him we can get that sorted out by Daddy and Mr. Craig," Colin said. "They'll know what to do. Finding him's what matters."

It would be disappointing if they couldn't bring Laddie back with them, Janet thought; she'd imagined them leading him home and having him there for Mr. Timms tomorrow. But of course if the man who'd got him had paid for him they could hardly take him away. But grown ups would be able to arrange it and Mr. Timms would have Laddie back quite soon. It was far better than having to say he was lost.

Tillmouth seemed a long way and they had to go by the main road which was horrid to ride along. They went in single file and cars dashed by all the time, some giving the ponies very little room. They stopped and bought sausage rolls, doughnuts and chocolate, also some Coca-Cola to drink, and they had their lunch going along. They could only jog-trot or walk so it didn't delay them.

At last they reached the outskirts of Tillmouth. They went through the town to the sea front, keeping to the side streets to avoid the traffic.

"Tide's nearly up," said Colin when they came out beside the sea. "Gosh, it'd be smashing to bathe."

"I don't see any ponies," said Janet.

There was very little sand left uncovered, and it was crowded with people. There were a lot of bathers too and the water looked very tempting.

"Let's ask," said Susan. She pulled up and spoke to a woman with two children who was passing. "Please, could you tell me if there are donkeys on the beach?"

"Oh yes, a man hires them out. He's just got some ponies too. My kiddies have a ride most days. Right along at the end——" she pointed.

Susan thanked her and they trotted along the sea front. The beach was much less crowded farther from the town and they saw, on the narrow strip of sand, a group of donkeys and ponies.

"It's them!" cried Janet.

"Is Laddie there?" asked Paul.

"I can't see yet. He *must* be!" She jumped off her bike and left it against some railings. Then she went down on to the beach and began to run towards the ponies.

CHAPTER NINE

"ABSOLUTELY FULL STOP!"

THERE were two grey donkeys and two brown ones. And beyond them stood three ponies. A large, bay, cobby animal, a little pie-bald Shetland and a chestnut. "It's Laddie!" shrieked Janet.

"Are you sure?" asked Susan. "Gosh, how marvellous!"

Janet was hugging his neck. "Of course I'm sure. I know him as well as anything. The way this bit of mane always goes over on the wrong side. And he's got a tiny little nick in his left ear. See it? This is Laddie all right. Oh, how simply super!"

"And our clues were right, we worked them out right," Paul said. "Jolly good sleuthing, I call it."

"It is rather," said Colin. "I was beginning to think we were sunk and would never find him. You and Sue did the best bits, Jan, over the clue of the red blazer."

"Jan," said Paul. "The donkeys have their names on their browbands. It looks smashing. I'd rather like to have Tom Thumb on Tommy's browband."

"Jolly nice," replied Janet without paying any

attention. *They'd found Laddie.* That was all that mattered. Now they only had to get him home before Mr. Timms came out of hospital tomorrow.

"Want a ride, miss?" asked the man who hired out the donkeys and ponies. He had been looking at them, and their ponies, in a puzzled way.

"No thank you," Janet replied. "But this is Mr. Timms' pony, Laddie. He lost him. Where did you find him?"

"Find 'im? I didn't find 'im," the man said indignantly. "What d'ye take me for? A thief? I bought 'im." He was a tall, dark man with a rather red face. Just now he was looking cross. He had a blue and white checked shirt, not very clean, with a red scarf tucked into the neck which gave him a gypsyish look. His voice was very loud.

"But where was he?" asked Janet, so pleased at finding Laddie that she didn't stop to think of the best way of asking the man without offending him.

"That's none o' your business," he answered angrily.

"We've been looking for him because we thought he'd strayed," Colin explained. "How did he get here?"

"Now look," said the man in an exasperated voice. "It's nothing to do with you. I bought that flipping pony from a local chap. And I paid for 'im, see?"

"Who? Was it Ted Deakins?" asked Colin.

The man roared, "Clear out. Comin' round asking a lot o' cheeky questions as if I'd pinched the flipping pony. Go on. 'Op it."

"Why?" asked Paul idiotically.

"Because I'm tired and sick o' your flipping questions. Go on, get out."

"I'm awfully sorry if we annoyed you but we've been looking for Laddie for ages——" Janet began when a woman with two little girls came up and asked the price of the donkey rides.

"Ninepence, lady. Ponies a shilling," said the man in a different sort of voice altogether, quite polite and pleasant. "Which'll you have, me dear?"

One of the children chose a grey donkey and the other one asked if she could ride Laddie. The man lifted them on, put their feet in the stirrups and gave them the reins to hold. Then a boy led each one and they moved off slowly, holding on to the front of the saddles and looking very happy. It was rather awful seeing Laddie working as a seaside pony because it seemed so final. They'd never get him back for Mr. Timms.

"If you ain't going to have rides, clear out," said the man crossly. Turning to one of the boys helping him he said, "Johnny, didn't I buy that chestnut pony, only last week?"

"Yes. Yer bought 'im. That's right," said the boy, who looked rather shabby and had a cigarette hanging from one corner of his mouth.

Janet was watching Laddie who was trotting slowly with the boy running beside him and holding the little girl. It wasn't hard work and he looked well. But what would Mr. Timms say when he knew?

"Come on, let's beat it," Colin said in an undertone. "Good afternoon," he said civilly but the man did not reply.

They went slowly away. The ponies looked about them with interest at the people and the sea, which was quite close for the tide was nearly right up.

As soon as they were out of hearing distance from the man Janet burst out, "He *is* mean. Not letting us have Laddie. He hardly listened when we tried to tell him about Mr. Timms and then he got cross. What *can* we do now?" She was nearly crying with disappointment.

"I don't know," Colin said slowly. "It wasn't any good staying and arguing with him. We can't prove anything."

They halted and stood looking at the group of donkeys and ponies. There was Laddie, the chestnut pony they had worked so hard to find, but they could not take him back to his paddock for Mr. Timms' return tomorrow.

"I wish we'd got our bathing kit. The sea looks smashing," said Paul. No one took any notice, things were too serious.

"There's hardly any sand left so I suppose they'll pack it in," Colin said. "They can't work very long, except at low tide."

"And Laddie looks well," said Susan. She was trying to make the best of things to cheer up Janet.

"But we've *got* to get him *home* by *tomorrow*," Janet cried frenziedly. "We *must*!"

"If that man won't even listen to us without getting annoyed——" Susan said doubtfully.

"Guilty conscience!" Colin stated. "He knows that Ted Deakins had stolen Laddie, I bet! We jolly well won't give up now."

Janet's spirits rose a little at this. "That's what I think. After all, we've found him. Shall we go back and ask the man to sell him to us?"

"Or grab him and gallop away?" suggested Paul.

"Could we?" asked Janet.

"No," said Susan.

"It'd be smashing, if it came off," Colin said, "but we'd have to be frightfully quick so they couldn't stop us." He looked across the narrow strip of sand to where the ponies and donkeys stood. "That boy holds the reins all the time, I don't think we could do it. And they could chase us on that cob."

"Super!" said Paul.

"But I don't think it'd come off and then we'd have made the man crosser still," Colin said.

"Buying Laddie's the only way," Susan said.

"No matter how much the man wants." Janet was very emphatic. "Even if it's pounds and pounds. Mummy would give it and I'd pay it back. Christmas and birthday presents and saving my pocket money."

"We could earn some," said Susan. They were walking back towards Laddie. "It'd be worth working all the hols to buy Laddie."

"We'll raise it somehow," Colin said. Janet found her friends' support very cheering as they went across to the man, though her heart sank at the thought of having to ask him about Laddie again. "Could you do it, Colin? He was annoyed with me. I put him in a bate."

"Sue would be best at it," he said. "People seem to give her things."

"I'll probably muck it up," Susan said uneasily.

"Say Mr. Timms is ill in hospital and doesn't know Laddie's missing," Janet advised, "so we want to buy him. That's all."

"All!" muttered Susan as they came up to where the man stood with his ponies and donkeys. They were preparing to leave as the tide was nearly covering all the sand. He gave them a sharp look as if to say, You again?

Susan smiled sweetly and went straight to the point. "Please, how much would you sell us the chestnut pony for?"

He stared in surprise. Then he said gruffly, "He ain't for sale."

"Oh, but *please*," begged Susan. "It's awfully important for us to have him. You see, he belongs to an old man who's in hospital and he doesn't know his pony has got lost."

"He's coming home tomorrow and he'll be frightfully upset when he finds his pony's not there," said Janet, unable to resist joining in.

The man pushed back his cap and scratched his head. "Blow me if I know what's got into yer about this flipping pony. It's just an ordinary pony."

"It's not. He's Mr. Timms' Laddie," insisted Janet. "He drives him in a cart and sells vegetables. That's how he earns his living."

"I can't 'elp that. He's mine now. And I didn't steal 'im." The man glared at Janet who said hurriedly, "I'm sure you didn't. He was lost—he strayed I expect."

"Now look, yer can't 'ave this pony. I'm not selling 'im. So 'op it. Clear off." The man sounded angry again. Then he turned to the boys who helped him and said, "Time we went. Come on." He went in front leading the cob and one of the donkeys and the boys followed with the others. Laddie came quite close as they went past and the boy who was leading him, and smoking a cigarette, looked at Janet cheekily. He was holding the reins firmly and she thought they would have no chance of snatching it away and galloping off. It was dreadful to see Laddie going away.

They watched them go up across the shingle and up on to the road. The water was coming up over the last little bit of sand and Midnight put his nose down and blew through his nostrils. A little wave curled round his fetlocks and he began to fidget.

"It'd be fun to ride out into the sea," Paul said.

"No time for fun. Laddie's the thing," Colin said. "I'm not going to be dished now, after all that sleuthing. There must be some way."

"We'll be drowned if we stay here," Susan pointed out. Everyone else had left the beach and were either sitting on the shingle above the high water mark or had gone home to tea. They went on to the road, the shingle crunched under the ponies' hooves and Midnight played up, pretending he was scared.

Janet recovered her bicycle. "Now what?" she asked.

"If only we'd proof he was Mr. Timms' pony," Colin said. "Then we could get the police to do something about it."

"Could they make that man give him up if he'd bought him?" Susan asked.

"I don't know. I vote we try the police," Colin answered. "Though they may not believe us without proof."

"Daddy rang them up," Janet began. "I know," she went on, "we'll ring Daddy and ask him to get on to the police again. Pr'aps he'd come over. He said he'd do anything he could to help." She looked at her watch. "Oh darn it! He won't be home yet. Shall I ring Mummy and ask her to ring him at the office and get him to come straight here? He'd be more likely to do it if she asked him. And I could explain we'll be rather late getting home."

"That seems a sound idea," Colin said. "I think we ought to let them know what's happening because we may be ages getting the police to go and see the man and everything."

"And Mummy will worry if we're very late," said Susan. "There's a telephone box just down the road."

"Anyone got any money?" Janet asked as they went towards it. Nobody had, it had all been spent on lunch.

"Not to worry," Colin said. "Just ask the operator to reverse the charge. I do if I ring up from school, only Dad gets annoyed if I do it too often as it goes on his telephone bill."

Janet went into the telephone box which was very hot and had quite a lot of sand on the floor, besides empty cigarette packets and ice-cream tubs. She gave the Deneway number and asked the operator to reverse the charge. She had never done this before and she wondered if her father would mind. While she waited, she thought about Mr. Timms coming home tomorrow. Would they get Laddie back in time? Surely if her father came and went to the Tillmouth police—she became aware that the bell was ringing and ringing, her mother must be out. The operator told her there was no reply and Janet thought crossly, As if I didn't know.

"Mummy isn't there," she told the others. "Could you try your mother?"

"Okay." Colin handed her Midnight's reins.

"It was beastly and hot in there," Janet said. "It is sickening to have so nearly got Laddie. I keep thinking of Mr. Timms coming home and finding out that he's lost. He'll have looked forward so much to seeing him."

"It might even make him ill again," Susan said seriously.

"I daresay he'll have saved up his sugar for him," said Janet mournfully, "though he doesn't think tit-bits are good for ponies, except as treats sometimes."

Colin came out of the telephone box letting the door slam behind him. "Whew! The heat in there!"

"What did she say?" Janet asked eagerly.

"We're to go home now and talk to Daddy, or Janet's father, about it before we do anything."

"Oh," said Janet disappointedly. To go home,

leaving Laddie behind, was like giving up. She had so hoped they could take him home with them.

"They can probably get the police to do more than we could," Colin said, mounting Midnight. "Though it's rather rotten that we can't finish the job ourselves, after sleuthing successfully."

"I don't really see how the man could be made to sell Laddie if he doesn't want to—I mean if he bought him without knowing he wasn't really Ted Deakins's to sell," Susan said.

"If they can't make him, it's absolutely full stop for us," Colin said. "In fact, I'm afraid it may be."

Susan said, "You ride Gallant, Jan. You biked most of the way here."

"I honestly don't mind." Janet was too miserable to care. She'd thought they were going to get Laddie back today. They'd solved the clue of the red blazer and they'd found him. Now they were, as Colin said, at an absolute full stop.

They jogged along the road towards Tillmouth until they were near the town and Colin said, "We'll turn off here and try to keep on the outside, so as not to get mixed up with the traffic."

They turned up a narrow road with small houses along one side and allotments on the other. It went in the right direction and before long Janet saw a path running along one side of the allotments which looked like a short cut. "Shall we go along here?" she suggested.

"Do let's," Paul said. "It's quite stony and one of the ponies might get a stone in his hoof. I've got my knife."

"It's unkind to try and make them pick up a stone," Susan objected.

"Not if I take it out at once." Paul began to ride up the path and they followed him.

CHAPTER TEN

RESCUE WORK

THE path was narrow so they rode in single file. Paul led, Colin came next, with Janet behind him. Susan was last, walking and pushing the bicycle.

On the one side were the allotments, fenced off from the path by railings, and on the other side there was a small paddock with a building standing in it. Janet saw at once that it was a wooden building which was stabling, she knew by the half doors that they were loose boxes. The paddock was rather bare and eaten down. Then she saw some donkeys, two brown ones and two grey.

"Hi! Look," she called. "This must be where that man keeps his ponies. There are the donkeys."

They stopped to look and Susan said, "Donkeys are rather sweet."

There was nobody about and the stables were shut up, no ponies looking out over the doors. The donkeys were eating at little heaps of hay scattered about in the paddock. It was tantalizing to think that Laddie was there, so close, and not in his own field just a few miles away, when Mr. Timms was coming home tomorrow.

"He does them well, at any rate," Colin said. "There's very little keep but they've got hay though it is summer. I expect that's why the ponies are stabled, because the field's so small and there's not much grass."

"We ought to go," Susan said, "or we'll be awfully late getting home."

"That beastly main road, we can't hurry," grumbled Paul, making Tom Thumb walk on.

Colin stayed, staring at the stables. "Here! Look!" he called urgently and they all turned to see what he meant. "Smoke. Coming from under the roof. See? Gosh! It must be on fire."

"The ponies! They must be inside," exclaimed Susan.

"Laddie!" shrieked Janet, getting off Gallant. "We *must* save him."

"We'll try." Colin hitched Midnight's reins over the allotments' railings. "Paul, dash back to that telephone box we passed and ring the Fire Brigade. Tell them the fire's opposite the allotments."

"Why me?" Paul objected. "I want to help."

"Because you're smallest and can do least here. Go on," ordered Colin, climbing over the fence into the paddock. "And get a move on."

"Can I dial 999?"

"Yes. Buck up," Colin shouted over his shoulder as he ran towards the stables.

"Go on, Paul! Hurry," called Susan. She had taken Gallant's reins from Janet and was hitching them over the railings beside Midnight. Even in her hurry she remembered to slip them under the cross bar and then over the post so that he could not shake it free.

Paul trotted back on the way they had come and Janet and Susan followed Colin, scrambling over the fence and then racing across the grass. Susan said in a worried voice, "It's made of wood so it'll burn awfully fast."

"I wonder which is Laddie's box," said Janet.

"I hope they're not locked," Colin exclaimed as they reached the four loose boxes. Smoke was curling out from under the eaves and there was an alarming sound of crackling. "The fire's worst in this one." He was pulling back the bolt of the door. "Look out, the metal's hot."

Janet darted to the next door. In her haste her fingers seemed clumsy and the bolt was stiff but at last it shot back and she pulled open the top half of the door. As she did so the draught fanned the fire, the crackling increased and smoke filled her eyes. For a minute she could not see anything. Then the smoke cleared a little and she saw Laddie. She plunged in and went up to him. He was standing still and shivering violently with fright.

"Come on, Laddie. Good boy, it's all right." She tried to soothe him by speaking quietly but her heart was bumping and she felt very frightened. She took hold of his forelock and tugged him but he stood as still as a rock. "Come *on*, Laddie." Janet felt like crying. He'd burn if she couldn't make him move for the roof was on fire and the stable was horribly hot already. But he wouldn't move.

Susan was shouting her name from the door and Janet went to her, choking and with her eyes streaming. "It's ghastly in there and Laddie won't move," she spluttered. She took a gulp of fresh air which felt lovely after the smoke.

Colin appeared beside them. "The tack's in this box next to Laddie and it's blazing. Lucky it's not a pony in there. Sue, can you get the cob out of the end one? I'm trying to make the Sheltie budge from the box by the tack room."

"How? What'll we do?" Janet almost sobbed.

"Something wet over our faces and their heads," Colin said quickly. "There's a tap here. I know, our jerseys." He stripped off his pullover and his shirt and soaked them under the tap. Then he put his pullover on his head and pulled it down over his face. Janet and Sue did the same with their jerseys.

Janet could see dimly through it and, as Colin disappeared into the loose box on the right of the burning one, she went back to the one on the left where Laddie was.

She hesitated in the doorway. The crackling was louder and she hated the sound of it. The smoke was worse too. No time to be lost, she thought, and she set her teeth and went in. It was stiflingly hot but the wet stuff over her face stopped the smoke from choking her and filling her eyes. As she groped her way towards Laddie Susan joined her. "I got the cob out. Colin gave me his shirt to put over his head and it did the trick."

"Hope it does with Laddie," Janet muttered, trying not to breathe in smoke. It was much better now she had Sue with her and she wasn't alone. She patted Laddie. "You *must* come, Laddie."

"Whoa, boy!" Susan's voice was muffled by her jersey. She raised the wet shirt to drape it over Laddie's head. They must hurry, Janet thought frenziedly, although the wet clothes over their faces made it easier to breathe the heat was almost unbearable. It was getting worse every minute and the crackling was louder. To leave Laddie was unthinkable but they couldn't possibly bear it for more than two or three minutes.

Laddie jerked his head away and began to back. He was sweating and shivering but he was too panic-stricken to go through the smoke to the door and safety.

"Get tough," Susan shouted. "Hang on to his

head, Jan. Stand *still*, Laddie." She tore at the shirt and ripped it open down the front to open it out and make it larger. Janet seized his forelock and grasped his neck firmly with the other hand. Susan slipped the shirt over his neck and pulled it forward over his eyes and down over his head. Janet moved her hand from his forelock and grasped a handful of mane. The damp cloth was a relief to him and when he could no longer see the smoke he lost some of his fear. "Come on," Janet coaxed and pulled.

"Go on," Susan said sharply and gave him a hard slap on his hind quarters.

He took a step forward. "He's coming," yelled Janet tugging hard at his mane. "Come on, Laddie!" A small piece of burning wood fell from the roof close to her and she stamped on the straw as it sparked alight. "Come on," she said desperately, she knew she couldn't endure the smoke and heat much longer. And if the burning roof fell in on them—she pulled at Laddie and Susan beat him with both hands.

Suddenly he began to walk forward. Slowly because he was blinded by the shirt but Janet hung on to his neck and guided him. He was trusting her and she was going to get him to safety.

As soon as his head was in the fresh air he went off with a rush and nearly knocked Janet over. The shirt fell off his head and Laddie cantered away to join the cob and the donkeys who were huddled together in a corner of the field.

"Heavenly to be outside," Susan said pulling off her jersey and coughing.

"Heaven!" Janet agreed, rubbing her smarting eyes. "And marvellous to have got Laddie out. I thought he never would come."

Colin came out of the smoke. "Well done!" he shouted. The crackle of the flames was very loud. "I can't shift the beastly Sheltie. Can you help?"

"Back into that?" groaned Janet. They wetted their jerseys and the shirt again under the tap for the heat had dried them. Then they pulled them on. "Hurry," yelled Colin. "The whole thing's going to go up any minute. If the roof falls in we've had it. We've got to get the Sheltie out."

The loose box in which the tack had been kept, and which was between Laddie's box and the little Shetland's, was blazing. Smoke and flames came through the window, which had fallen in, and Janet saw little flames licking up under the eaves of the roof. It was made of wood and covered with black roofing felt which melted in the heat and which the flames seemed to devour. And there was a pony in there which they had got to rescue.

They groped their way into the loose box. Janet and Susan held hands so as to keep close together. The heat met them as soon as they were inside the door and they stopped. They *couldn't* go into that.

"Got to get him out or he'll be burnt," gasped Colin.

Poor little Sheltie, thought Janet, if they could dash in and get him quickly—she went after Colin and Susan was beside her.

The pony was too terrified to move or struggle when Susan put the wet shirt over his head and held it in place under his throat.

"Push him," Colin shouted. It was hard to hear what he said in the crackling din and with his voice, and her ears, muffled but Janet made out what he meant and joined him in pushing the Shetland's hindquarters. "Shove," panted Colin and Janet stooped and pushed. Nearer the floor the air was less hot and the smoke less dense. She no longer felt she was choking but the heat was getting worse all the time.

They put their shoulders against the round, plump hindquarters and they felt the Shetland stiffen as he resisted. Susan was tugging him by his mane but he would not move.

Colin stamped out a piece of burning straw. "Join hands behind him and heave. It's the only hope," he said, through a fit of coughing.

They clasped their hands above the little pony's hocks and pulled. How strong ponies were, Janet thought, her clothes were sticking to her with the heat and she thought she couldn't stand much more. But they couldn't give up and leave the pony and she wasn't going to be the first to give in. But supposing the roof fell on them? Suppose they couldn't get out? Fear must have given them strength for they almost lifted the Shetland's hind-quarters off the ground and he took a step forward.

Once he had started they could keep him moving. They hustled him along with their hands joined round his hind legs. Slowly and reluctantly he reached the door. Susan whipped off the shirt and the pony stopped dead.

"Go on," roared Colin. He and Janet gave a terrific heave and the pony shot forward and out of the door. He trotted off snorting with fright. Then he neighed, one of the ponies answered and the little Shetland scuttled off to join them.

Susan, Janet and Colin pulled the clothes off their heads. Their eyes were streaming and they felt as if they had swallowed a lot of smoke.

"I took the shirt off his head too soon," Susan coughed.

"Get clear of this," said Colin and they walked away from the heat of the burning stable, mopping their eyes and coughing. Once they were in the fresh air they felt better at once.

"We saved them," Janet said thankfully.

CHAPTER ELEVEN

"999!"

"THANK goodness we got them out without anyone being hurt," said Susan.

"It was a pretty close thing. We couldn't have stayed in there much longer," said Colin.

Janet looked at one of her sandals, a little hole was burnt through the sole. "I thought my foot felt hot. The wet things over our faces made all the difference. We couldn't have stuck it otherwise."

"We had a talk at school about it," Colin explained. "Really you should go into a burning room on your hands and knees to drag anyone out, because the air's clearer low down."

"That obstinate little Sheltie! I thought he never would budge. Poor little thing, he was scared stiff," said Susan. "Oh, here's Paul."

He came rushing up. "The fire engine's coming! I phoned. I dialled 999. They wouldn't believe me at first. Gosh! It isn't half going up in smoke."

They turned and looked at the stable which was really blazing. "We rescued the ponies," Susan told him with triumph. "We got them out. But it was an awful job."

"I wish I'd been here, it must have been terrifically exciting. But I did dial 999!" Paul said.

"It wasn't exciting, it was ghastly!" said Janet. "It was so horribly hot. And I was frightened we wouldn't get the ponies out."

"They wouldn't move," Susan said. "It was awful."

"Here's the fire engine!" Paul shouted, and they all heard the bell clanging in the distance. Colin said anxiously, "I don't think it'll be able to get up this narrow lane."

The sound of the bell came nearer and Paul shouted, "Here it is! Coming into the field." They had not noticed a gate on the far side of the paddock and now they saw the fire engine was coming through it. Shining and red, with firemen in helmets, it bumped across the grass. The men were off it and unrolling a huge hose almost before it had stopped. They had a water tank on tow behind the engine and in no time they were playing water on the stable.

"Nobody inside? No animals?" asked one of the firemen, who seemed to be in charge. Colin said he was the officer.

"No, we got them out," Susan said proudly.

"Well done!"

There was a glorious hissing sound, much nicer

than the horrid crackling, as the hose played water on the stable roof, quenching the flames and dripping from the eaves.

"Gosh, how smashing!" said Paul. "I'd like to be a fireman."

"Here's the man they belong to," exclaimed Susan, and they looked round. He was hurrying towards them and his red face was quite pale. "It's all right," Susan called. "They're safe."

He was so out of breath he could hardly speak for a minute. Then he panted, "Thank 'eaven for that. 'Cor, I couldn't 'ardly believe my ears when I 'eard as it was on fire. And them three ponies in there. Who got 'em out? The Fire Brigade chaps?"

"No. We did. They wouldn't have been here in time," Colin told him. "We only just did it."

He looked at them. "Well! I wouldn't 'ave believed you could. How did ye shift 'em? 'Orses won't go through fire or smoke, 'orses won't."

"It was an awful job, they wouldn't budge," said Janet.

"The cob was the easiest, he was farthest away from the fire. It started in the stable where you kept your tack," Colin explained. "We'd a frightful time getting the Shetland to move."

"Stubborn little blighters!" The man mopped his forehead with a very grubby handkerchief. " 'Ow d'ye get 'em to move?"

"We soaked our jerseys, and my shirt, and put

them ovcr our faces. And the shirt over their heads," Colin told him. "Otherwise we'd never have managed it."

"And we practically lifted the Sheltie off his feet, with our hands joined round his hind legs," said Janet.

"A good way to make 'em move. Fancy you knowing that," said the man.

"The chap who drove our horse-box the other day told me about it," Colin explained. "And I suddenly remembered."

"You sure have got yer 'eads screwed on the right way," the man said admiringly and Paul pretended to feel his to see if it would unscrew. "Wet things over yer faces and something over the nags' 'eads. 'Cor, that was real smart."

"We had a talk about fire fighting at school," said Colin.

"I never learnt nothing so useful when I was a nipper at school. Who sent for the fire engine?"

"I did." Paul said proudly. "I dialled 999."

"Yer the best bunch o' kids I ever came across," he declared. And Janet thought he was quite different now, friendly and really rather nice. Could it be possible that he might be persuaded to sell Laddie to them at the end of the summer? Dare she ask and risk making him cross again?

"If any o' them ponies 'ud come to any 'arm," he was saying, "I'd never 'ave got over it." He turned to Janet. "If you still want the chestnut pony yer can 'ave 'im."

"Can I really?" cried Janet, hardly able to believe it. "Thank you most frightfully. How absolutely marvellous!" Laddie was not only saved but he would be going home to Mr. Timms. "How much will he be?" she asked, suddenly remembering this.

"No charge, not to you," he said emphatically. "Why, if yer'd not got 'em out—'cor, it don't do to think of, do it?"

They all agreed that it didn't.

"But I think we ought to pay you for him," Susan said seriously. "Because you must have bought him and you didn't know he belonged to Mr. Timms."

"Too right I didn't. But 'smatter of fact I had him off my brother and he didn't make no charge to me. I might 've guessed Ted wouldn't give anything away unless there was something screwy about it. He's that sort."

"Ted Deakins?" asked Colin. The man, Mr. Deakins as they now began to think of him, nodded. They all felt a glow of triumph for their sleuth work had been correct.

"Thank you awfully for letting us have Laddie," said Susan and Colin thanked him too, adding that it was very lucky they had gone along the path and seen the smoke coming from the stables. "I wonder how it started," Colin went on. "It must have begun in the tack room. That was burning the worst."

"Them darned boys smoking, I'll be bound," said Mr. Deakins angrily. "I've told the lot of 'em, dozens o' times, not to smoke in the stables. Them and their flipping cigarettes. 'Cor, I'll wallop 'em for this. They won't sit comfortable when I've done with 'em!" Paul giggled and Colin grinned, even Susan couldn't feel sorry for them and Janet felt quite glad they would be punished. Nobody who had seen the ponies' fright, and felt the heat, would ever forget it. How lucky it was that she had suggested taking a short cut and Paul had wanted to ride along the stony path. And if Colin hadn't noticed the smoke—she gave a little shiver. As Mr. Deakins said, it didn't do to think about it.

"It's practically out now," said Colin. The stable was wet and blackened. Most of the roof was burnt away and so were parts of the walls between the tack room and the loose boxes on either side.

"If ever I have a stable no one will be allowed to smoke near it," said Janet solemnly.

The firemen were rolling up their hoses and the officer came across to speak to Mr. Deakins. After he went back to the engine it drove away and they watched it go out through the gate. Then Mr. Deakins said, "Going to take that chestnut pony with you?"

"Please," said Janet. "I say, I'm awfully sorry you have lost all your tack."

"Got to manage some'ow," he said, almost cheerfully. "Dunno where'll I find to keep 'em that's near the town. This was all I could get to rent. I'd rather have 'em all turned out at night but I couldn't get a big enough field. One pony less'll be all to the good with them being a bit crowded."

"How can we manage without a halter?" Janet asked.

"If you wait a little I'll fix you up," Mr. Deakins said. "Just get a bit o' rope and I'll soon make one."

"Thank you awfully," Janet said. "Mr. Timms is coming out of hospital tomorrow and he doesn't know that Laddie got lost. He'd have been terribly upset as he's awfully fond of him. He got out and strayed away, you see."

"We sleuthed and traced him," said Paul.

"We'll be awfully late getting home," Susan said rather anxiously and with a glance at where their ponies were waiting patiently. "Golly, we are in a mess too."

They had been too busy to notice but now they looked at each other and saw they were all as dirty as chimney sweeps, dark smears on their faces, their clothes streaked with black and Janet had a hole burnt in one of her sandals.

"Did it burn your foot too?" asked Paul.

"I never noticed. Things were so hectic," she replied.

Colin had no shirt to wear but luckily it was a very warm day and he often went without one, nor did they mind not being able to wear their jerseys. Mr. Deakins soon came back with a length of rope which he made into a halter for Laddie and they set off home with Janet riding Gallant and leading Laddie in triumph. They could hardly believe it was true that they were taking him home.

Mrs. Fenton greeted them with cries of dismay. "My dear children, what have you been doing? You are very late and I was getting anxious. You're black!"

"We've been fire-fighting," said Colin.

"I dialled 999," Paul boasted.

"We saved Laddie and two other ponies," Janet explained and Susan said reassuringly, "It's all right, Mummy, we didn't get hurt or anything."

"And we got Laddie back for Mr. Timms," said Janet. She felt very tired now.

"The fire engine came. It was smashing. I'm going to be a fireman," said Paul.

"Wash yourselves quickly and come and have something to eat," said Mrs. Fenton. She insisted on Janet staying for supper—it was supper time by now—and rang up Mrs. Craig to say she would bring her back in the car.

"Thank you." Janet thought it would be nice not to have to bicycle home. "But I must take Laddie back."

"Leave him here for tonight," Mrs. Fenton suggested. So they turned him out with Midnight, Gallant and Tom Thumb and they all started at once to eat furiously.

After supper Janet went home. She had a splendid story to tell her mother and father. They were very glad to hear that Laddie had been found in time for Mr. Timms' return but her mother was horrified at the thought of them going into a burning stable. "Very plucky, though," said her father. Janet went happily to bed.

CHAPTER TWELVE

MR. TIMMS COMES HOME

"THERE'S an awful lot of grass, I hope he doesn't blow himself out and get colic," said Colin.

"He'll get very fat," Susan remarked.

"I wish Mr. Timms would buck up and come," said Janet. They were all leaning on the gate of the paddock and watching Laddie who had just been turned out in his own field again. He had walked round as if he were inspecting it to see that everything was all right. Then he had rolled and after that he had begun to graze.

Colin had mended the weak place in the hedge which, they thought, was where Laddie had got out.

"To think Mr. Timms is coming back today and we only got Laddie here this morning," Janet said. She could still hardly believe that they had really recovered him in time.

"In the nick of time," said Paul impressively.

"Shall we have a look at the cottage?" suggested Janet. "Mrs. Chandler, she's the woman from a village near Trewsbury, and she's awfully nice, has got it ready. And Mummy sent some things she'd cooked all ready for Mr. Timms. I'm afraid the garden must be rather untidy. It's a shame as Mr. Timms keeps it beautifully and he's so proud of his flowers."

"We might have come and weeded it if we'd thought," Susan said sorrowfully.

"Sleuthing took up most of our time," Colin pointed out.

"The banner looks nice, though," said Paul. It hung on the paddock gate, an old piece of sheet with the words "Welcome Home" in red letters. The letters had started too big and were squeezed up at the end, and the red ink had run a little. But it looked fine and very welcoming.

"Now sleuthing's done, we'll have time to bathe every day," Colin said.

"I still haven't used my knife to take a stone out of a hoof," Paul complained.

They walked across the lane to the cottage and opened the garden gate. "Goodness!" exclaimed Janet. "Who's done this weeding?"

Mrs. Chandler appeared at the front door and flapped a duster. Then she said, "Oh, I thought it was Mr. Timms come. I've the kettle on already for a cup of tea for him. And some dinner in the oven."

"It's jolly good of you," said Janet.

"Oh well, we're put into this world to help each other. That's what I always say," said Mrs.

Chandler cheerfully. "And the poor old man's all on his own."

"Who did the garden?" Janet asked. "I wish we'd thought of doing it."

"Well, my dear, you've done your bit getting that pony back. What Mr. Timms would have done if he'd come home and found that blessed pony gone I don't know! He sets such store by him. Now if it'd been a cat I could have understood it. Ever so fond of my Tibby, I am."

"Oh, Mrs. Chandler," said Janet, shocked at anyone liking cats better than ponies, though Goloshes was sweet. "Ponies are much the best."

"It takes all sorts to make a world," said Mrs. Chandler, smiling. "It was my hubby that did the garden, came along one or two evenings and tidied it up."

"It looks lovely," said Janet. It really did. There were lots of bright flowers, and there wasn't a weed to be seen. Then Janet remembered something else. "Laddie's tack. It'll be all mildewy. We could clean it."

"No time," said Colin. "Here's the car."

It came slowly up the lane and drew up at the garden gate. A small, spare man got out and thanked the driver. He stood looking round, holding a small suitcase.

"Hello, Mr. Timms," said Janet. "I'm awfully glad you're better and home again."

"Thank you. I'm fine. Made a new man o' me, they did," answered Mr. Timms.

Susan, Colin and Paul looked at him with interest. He was very neat. He had the brightest blue eyes and grey hair. Janet introduced them. "They've all got ponies," she said.

"I'd like to see them," Mr. Timms said. "How are you, Mrs. Chandler? What's this? A committee to welcome me home?" he chuckled. Then he saw the banner. "Bless me, I never thought I'd get V.I.P. treatment! That's a real knock-out, that is!"

"You come along in and sit down and have a nice cup of tea," Mrs. Chandler said, speaking as if Mr. Timms was Paul's age.

"One thing I got to do first." Mr. Timms put down his suitcase and felt in his pocket. He brought out a handful of lump sugar. "Just got to see Laddie and give 'im a treat."

He walked across the lane to the paddock gate. Janet and Susan exchanged glances. They were both thinking how dreadful it would have been if Mr. Timms had found the paddock was empty. He had a good look at the banner which hung on the paddock gate and looked round at Janet. "You done this?" She nodded. "Nice of you, thanks. Now, where's that pony?" He raised his voice. "C-o-o-p boy." Laddie raised his head and looked towards the gate. Then he trotted across to Mr. Timms.

They watched Mr. Timms give him the sugar. He ran his hand along his neck, patted him and gently tweaked one ear. "Good old Laddie. He's looking fine." He turned to Janet and said, "You don't know how grateful I am to you for looking after him. I used to lie in bed and think about him and I was ever so glad I'd asked you to see to him. I knew you'd see he was all right."

Janet was much impressed. Mr. Timms who knew all about horses had relied on her and thought she was capable of looking after Laddie. How thankful she was she hadn't got to say he was lost. He would have to know all that had happened but she decided not to tell him everything just yet. Let him get settled down first. "Laddie got out of his field, but we got him back," she said. "I'll tell you about it when we've more time. Colin mended the place in the fence so it's all right now."

"Thanks," Mr. Timms said and then Mrs. Chandler broke in. "Mr. Timms you come in now and have a rest and a nice cuppa," she said firmly. "There'll be plenty of time to talk about that pony tomorrow. You want to take care of yourself till you're strong again."

He gave Laddie the last lump of sugar, patted him and then walked back to the garden gate. "Maybe yer right, Mrs. Chandler. I could do with a sit-down and a cuppa."

"We'll come and see you tomorrow and tell you

all the news," said Janet. "We're going to clean your tack for you as it's not been done for so long."

"You've no call to do that, thank you kindly; I've still got a bit o' life left in me. Bless me, who's been gardening? I was feared the weeds 'ud be all over."

"Mr. Chandler did it," said Janet. "We'll be along tomorrow to have a go at the tack. And we'll show you the ponies. They're simply super."

"Pleased, I'm sure." Mr. Timms smiled at the Fentons. "So you're all horsemen?"

"Sort of," said Colin. "I'd like to ask you how to stop Midnight, he's my pony, from hotting up when I jump him. He pulls my arms out sometimes. I wondered if I'm riding him in the wrong bit. Jan said you'd know."

"I'd like to see him." Mr. Timms was interested at once. "You need to get him jumping slowly over small things to steady him down. We might put up a little jump or two in my field and school him. School you, too!" Mr. Timms smiled at Colin.

Colin grinned back. "That'd be smashing. Thanks a lot."

They said good-bye and walked back to Deneway.

"I say, wasn't it lucky our sleuthing came off so well," said Susan. "Just think, if it hadn't!"

"Red rosettes for the Pony Sleuths!" said Paul.